Tacit and Ambiguous Resources as Sources of
Competitive Advantage

# Tacit and Ambiguous Resources as Sources of Competitive Advantage

Véronique Ambrosini

First published 2003 by
PALGRAVE MACMILLAN
Houndmills, Basingstoke, Hampshire RG21 6XS and
175 Fifth Avenue, New York, N.Y. 10010
Companies and representatives throughout the world

PALGRAVE MACMILLAN is the global academic imprint of the Palgrave Macmillan division of St. Martin's Press, LLC and of Palgrave Macmillan Ltd. Macmillan® is a registered trademark in the United States, United Kingdom and other countries. Palgrave is a registered trademark in the European Union and other countries.

ISBN 1–4039–0575–4

This book is printed on paper suitable for recycling and made from fully managed and sustained forest sources.

A catalogue record for this book is available from the British Library.

Library of Congress Cataloging in Publication Data
Ambrosini, Véronique.
   Tacit and ambiguous resources as sources of competitive
   advantage / Véronique Ambrosini.
      p.   cm.
   Includes bibliographical references and index.
   ISBN 1–4039–0575–4 (cloth)
      1. Intangible property—Management.   2. Tacit knowledge.   3. Ambiguity.
   4. Knowledge management.   5. Organisational learning.   6. Strategic
   planning.   I. Title.
   HD53.A43 2003
   658.4′038—dc21                                            2003043609

10   9   8   7   6   5   4   3   2   1
12   11   10   09   08   07   06   05   04   03

Printed and bound in Great Britain by
Antony Rowe Ltd, Chippenham and Eastbourne

# Contents

## PART V   IMPLICATIONS AND CONCLUSIONS

# List of Figures and Tables

**Figures**

## Tables

# Acknowledgements

I am indebted to many people for their assistance with this book. First of all I would like to express my gratitude to Professor Cliff Bowman for his invaluable help and support, and for being an outstanding mentor. Under his supervision and through his insights into strategic management, the organisational world and the art of writing academic papers I have been able to learn and develop as an academic. I would also like to say a particular thank you to Jon Billsberry and my mother for their support and confidence in me. Finally I would like to thank Professors Jenkins, McGee and Sims for their advice.

VERONIQUE AMBROSINI

# Introduction and Overview

The concept of tacit knowledge has received a good deal of attention in the strategy field, and particularly the resource-based view of the firm literature. It has been argued that tacit knowledge is of crucial importance to firms because it is a source of sustainable competitive advantage. However the attention dedicated to the phenomenon has been principally conceptual and there has been little empirical work to support this argument. The empirical research reported in this book was aimed at determining whether tacit knowledge was perceived by managers to be a component of their firm's success. Figure I.1 depicts the main stages of the study and also serves as summary of this book.

Part I of the book provides a description of the main principles of the resource-based view of the firm, reviews the tacit knowledge literature and refines the definition of tacit knowledge in order to make it empirically researchable, because 'if a construct is conceptually clear but empirically impossible to measure, then it is of limited utility in advancing our quest for knowledge' (Thomas and Pollock, 1999, p. 137). It is argued that organisational tacit knowledge should be defined as tacit routines, that is, as tacit organisational activities. Part II builds on this argument by emphasising the difference between individual tacit knowledge and organisational tacit knowledge and suggesting that there are different degrees of tacitness. Part II concludes by reiterating the aims of the research: to determine whether tacit activities are perceived by managers to be a component of their firm's success, and to establish the implications of tacit routines for the management of organisational success and for strategic management.

Part III is dedicated to methodology and proposes a method for empirically researching tacit routines: causal mapping aided by storytelling. Part IV discusses the empirical research and shows that tacit activities can indeed be seen as a component of firms' success. It also further refines the methodology and the concept of tacit knowledge as a source of sustainable competitive advantage. During the research it became evident that other types of routine also play an important part in organisational success: routines that are either ignored, not well understood, or known but their effect on performance is not known. Finally, Part V discusses the conceptual and managerial implications of the findings of the research. In particular it shows how different types

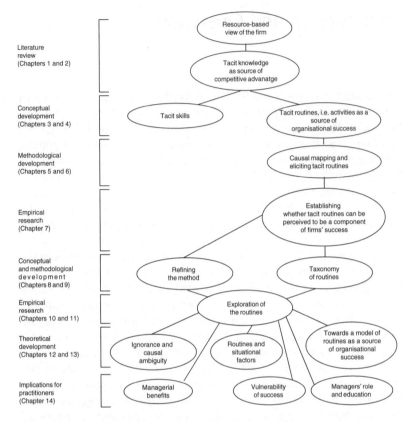

*Figure I.1* Tacit knowledge as a source of organisational success: a route map

of routine have different consequences for managerial tasks and for the sustainability of firms' success. It also highlights the benefits of eliciting tacit or not well understood routines, and explains that if managers become aware of these routines they can protect them and if appropriate enhance, transfer or change them.

# Part I

# Literature Review

# 1

# The Resource-Based View of the Firm

## Introduction

Until the early 1980s strategic management was strongly informed by neoclassical economics, and notably the structure–conduct–performance paradigm of industrial organisation economics (IO) (Caves and Porter, 1977; Caves, 1980; Porter, 1980). Broadly speaking the main thesis of IO is that competitive advantage derives from a privileged market position. It argues that the prime determinant of a firm's performance is its external environment – the structure of the industry to which it belongs. In other words, according to the IO perspective the source of a firm's profits is its market position, protected by barriers to entry into the market.

The resource-based view of the firm adopts a different approach. It states that a firm can be regarded as a bundle of resources (Rumelt, 1984; Amit and Shoemaker, 1993), and that these resources enable the firm to obtain a sustainable competitive advantage. In other words the resource-based view rests on the belief that competitive advantage does not depend on market and industry structures but on internal resources; that is, it locates the source of superior profitability inside the firm. The underlying assumptions of the resource-based view are that resources are heterogeneous across organisations, that firms differ with respect to their resources, and that there is asymmetry in firms' resource endowment. This heterogeneity can remain over time, which means that resource transferability is limited. Proponents of the view also assume that resources are not perfectly mobile across firms.

The resource-based view is based on Selznick's (1957) seminal work on 'distinctive competences' and on Penrose's (1959) argument that a firm is a collection of resources and its performance depends on its ability to use them. The later reformulation of the view can be traced to an article by Wernerfelt (1984), whose views were subsequently developed by Barney (1986) and Dierickx and Cool (1989). However the perspective really took off in the 1990s, when a number of conceptual papers were published (for example Barney, 1991; Conner, 1991; Mahoney and Pandian, 1992; Peteraf, 1993) and the principles were popularised by Prahalad and Hamel (1990; Hamel and Prahalad, 1994).

Although the resource-based view is a relatively recent phenomenon, it is worth noting that the perspective is very much consistent with the strategic management tradition as in essence it focuses on the strengths and weaknesses elements of the widely used SWOT analysis. Therefore it would be misleading to argue that the resource-based view is in opposition to IO or other economics-based perspectives, and it may be more appropriate to consider it as complementing other theories. Finally, although the 1990s saw an explosion of conceptual work in this area there are still very few empirical studies (see for instance Collis, 1991; Henderson and Cockburn, 1994; Miller and Shamsie, 1996), and while more theoretical work is needed, the future of the resource-based view lies very much in the search for empirical evidence. For instance there is a need to know more about the implementability of the view's principles and how to identify resources (Wernerfelt, 1984). There is also a need to know which resources are valuable in which contexts (Miller and Shamsie, 1996) and, on the more practical side, how resources can be managed in such a way as to remain or become sources of sustainable competitive advantage.

## Key principles

Barney's (1991) work on the principles of the resource-based view is key to the perspective. His main contributions have been to characterise what enables a resource to be a source of competitive advantage, and in so doing to highlight the importance of the intangible, hard-to-define elements that are found in organisations.

### What is a resource?

There is little controversy about what a resource is, and it is agreed that it can be almost anything. For instance it has been defined as 'anything which could be thought of as a strength or weakness of a given firm' (Wernerfelt, 1984, p. 172), and as 'those (tangible and intangible) assets which are tied semi-permanently to the firm' (ibid.) Resources can be categorised as physical resources (for example machinery, buildings), human resources (knowledge, experience, workers' insights), organisational resources (organisational culture, organisational structure, informal processes) or financial resources (debt, equity) (Barney, 1991).

It is worth noting that numerous terms are used to describe resources. They are variously called capabilities, strategic assets, organisational competences, and core competences (if a resource is a source of sustainable competitive advantage). Sometimes a distinction is made between resources and capabilities (Grant, 1991a; Amit and Shoemaker, 1993; Rao, 1994), sometimes it is not (Wernerfelt, 1984; Peteraf, 1993). When such a distinction is made, 'resource' is understood as resource possession and 'capability' as resource utilisation (Brumagim, 1994). That is, resources are seen as consisting of inputs into the production process, and capabilities as the processes by which the resources are utilised. In this book the term resources will encompass both resources and capabilities.

## Characteristics of a resource

The resource-based view does not propose that just any resource can be a source of competitive advantage. Rather it must possess a number of characteristics and these characteristics must hold simultaneously:

- Resources must be *valuable*. A resource is said to be valuable if 'it exploits opportunities and/or neutralises threats in a firm's environment', or if it 'enable[s] a firm to conceive of or implement strategies that improve its efficiency and effectiveness' (Barney, 1991, pp. 105, 106).
- Resources must be *rare*; that is, they must not be possessed by a large number of firms. Any resource that is possessed by a large number of firms cannot be a source of sustainable competitive advantage. Resources that are valuable but not scarce can only be sources of competitive parity (Barney, 1995). Some resources may be essential but they are only prerequisites in that they provide order-qualifying rather than order-winning product features. This does not imply that these resources do not matter. On the contrary they are needed by firms if they want to be players in the industry, if they are to compete and survive.
- Resources must be *imperfectly mobile*; that is not easily traded. If a resource can easily be bought and exchanged then it cannot be a source of difference and therefore cannot be a source of sustainable competitive advantage.
- Resources must be *imperfectly imitable*; that is, others firms cannot copy them and thereby obtain equivalent resources. Similarly an

organisation's resource does not have a 'differential ability' (Conner, 1994) if its competitors can copy it, for if they are able to do so the organisation's advantage will be nullified.

- Resources cannot have any strategically *equivalent substitutes*: if a resource can be easily substituted by another resource that delivers the same effect, then it cannot remain a source of competitive advantage.

It should be noted that authors often assume that all resources are valuable, and when employing the term resource they implicitly suggest that the resource is valuable despite the fact that it may also be dysfunctional. Thus some clarification of the term valuable in regard to the resource-based view of the firm is required (Bowman and Ambrosini, 2000a).

In summary, in order to be a source of sustainable competitive advantage a resource must be simultaneously unique, difficult to trade and difficult to duplicate and substitute. However knowing which characteristics are necessary for a resource to be a source of sustainable competitive advantage is only part of starting to understand resources. One also needs to appreciate what makes a resource rare, what restricts its mobility and what hinders its imitation.

Resources can be difficult to imitate for various reasons, but the most argued for reason is that organisations have 'isolating mechanisms' (Rumelt, 1984) that protect the organisation's resources from imitation and preserve the stream of profits or rents accruing to them. 'Causal ambiguity' is one such mechanism (Lippman and Rumelt, 1982). This relates to the uncertainty that 'stems from a basic ambiguity concerning the nature of the causal connections between actions and results, the factors responsible for performance differentials will resist precise identification' (ibid., p. 418). Causal ambiguity limits imitation and mobility because competitors do not know the causes of a rival firm's effectiveness, and therefore do not know what they should be imitating (Rumelt, 1987). Moreover it is often the case that a firm itself knows no better than its competitors the reasons for its competitive advantage, and therefore this advantage is likely to be sustained because imitation cannot take place. Barney (1991) implies that causal ambiguity can only be a real source of competitive advantage if firms ignore the link between their resources and their advantage, for if a firm can understand this link, then others can do so too. Other firms can just purchase the resources they need to reproduce the same effects, thereby acquiring the same advantage as the first firm. As a result the former loses its competitive advantage. Thus one conclusion is that competitive advantage can only be sustained if firms ignore its origin, because then replication is almost impossible. Lippman and Rumelt (1982, p. 420) acknowledge that immobility can frequently be explained by uniqueness but they state that uncertainty and uniqueness are independent, because 'in the absence of uncertainty, the creation of a unique resource could be repeated and its uniqueness destroyed'. They state that factors are immobile not because they are unique but because causal ambiguity means that they cannot be replicated.

While causal ambiguity is certainly one of the main reasons for a resource's inimitability and immobility, it is not the only one. There are also the following.

### Time compression diseconomies (Dierickx and Cool, 1989)

Some resources are imperfectly imitable because they are history-dependent. Factors such as routines, organisational culture, past investments and so on impact heavily on the development of resources. This is at the root of the suggestion that inimitability can stem from the difficulty of discovering and repeating the development processes that are responsible for a resource's existence.

### Asset mass efficiencies and the interconnectedness of asset stocks (Dierickx and Cool, 1989)

Resources can remain immobile and unable to be replicated or transferred because the initial level of an asset influences the pace of further accumulation, and because the accumulation of an existing asset depends not only on the level of that asset but also on the levels of others. The interconnectedness of asset stocks refers to a situation in which the 'lack of complementary assets can often impede a firm from accumulating an asset which it needs to serve its market successfully' (Verdin and Williamson, 1994, p. 87). For these reasons, replicating a resource can be extremely difficult.

All this means that history matters. As a firm develops it acquires resources, develops traditions and ways of doing things, and hence becomes unique. Its resources can be extremely difficult to imitate because their existence is due to the firm's unique history, the unique paths travelled (by the founder and employees, critical events and so on). It has the resources it has only because of the situations it has faced and how it has responded to them. Resource accumulation cannot be reproduced overnight and it may be impossible to reproduce it at all because circumstances can never be the same again.

## Specificity

Some resources 'are specialised to a particular usage or firm' (Castanias and Helfat, 1991, p. 162), and therefore cannot be fully copied. This can be understood by means of Nonaka's explanation that 'what makes sense in one context can change or even lose its meaning when communicated to people in a different context' (Nonaka, 1991, p. 103). This means that although some resources could be transferred from one organisation to another, their efficiency or effectiveness would not be as great as it was before because the context as a whole would be different.

## Codifiability

If a resource is tangible or if its structure is defined by a set of identifiable rules (Kogut and Zander, 1992) – that is, if it can be articulated (Winter, 1987) – then it can be easily imitated and consequently cannot be a source of sustained advantage.

The fact that a resources that is difficult to codify is a potential source of sustainable competitive advantage has led strategy researchers to argue that tacit knowledge plays a central part in the development of sustainable competitive advantage because it meets all the criteria that allow a resource to generate such an advantage. However, despite widespread agreement about and an ever growing body of literature on this argument, the idea has remained largely conceptual and there is little empirical evidence to support it. Hence there is a 'need to know much more empirically about the nature of tacit knowledge for it to become a theoretically . . . convincing construct' (Jensen, 1993, p. 9). Chapter 2 is devoted to defining and explaining tacit knowledge.

# 2
# Tacit Knowledge

## Tacit knowledge and the resource-based literature

As mentioned in Chapter 1, a number of authors have argued that tacit knowledge plays a central part in the development of sustainable competitive advantage (for example Badaracco, 1991; Nonaka, 1991; Grant, 1993; Spender, 1993; Sobol and Lei, 1994). Quinn (1992), Badaracco (1991) and Clark (1987) suggest that because of the dynamic conditions of the market, competitive advantage is no longer dependent on investment in machinery, on the attribute of products or on tangible resources as these can be purchased or replicated. Hence Grant (1993) asserts that knowledge, and notably tacit knowledge, is now firms' most strategically significant resource. He justifies this assertion by arguing, similarly to Quinn (1992), that because of the ability of competitors to acquire resources quickly the 'sustainability of competitive advantage . . . requires resources which are idiosyncratic . . . and not so easily transferable or replicable. The criteria point to knowledge (tacit knowledge in particular) as the most strategically-important resource of the firm' (Grant, 1993, p. 2). This opinion is shared by Sobol and Lei, who state that in the future firms will no longer compete on the attributes of their products but on the skills and capabilities they can deploy, so organisational learning and tacit knowledge will 'become the only renewable and sustainable base for a firm's activities. Tacit knowledge and skills are particularly important sources of future competitive advantage because they are difficult for competitors to see and imitate quickly' (Sobol and Lei, 1994, p. 177).

## Objective knowledge

Before going further into the discussion of tacit knowledge, how to research it and its implications, the concept needs to be defined. The customary way of doing so is to compare it to objective knowledge, which can 'be communicated from its possessor to another person in symbolic form and the recipient of the communication becomes as much "in the know" as the originator' (Winter, 1987, p. 171). This suggests that objective knowledge consists of two facets, the first of which is communicability: it can be readily 'written down, encoded, explained, or understood' (Sobol and Lei, 1994, p. 170). The second factor concerns its possession. Sobol and Lei argue that 'such knowledge is not specific or idiosyncratic to the firm or person possessing it' (ibid.) and therefore it can be shared. While this definition, or subtle variations of it, is widely used throughout the literature, numerous terms are used to refer to it: articulated knowledge (Hedlund, 1994), articulable knowledge (Winter, 1987), explicit knowledge (Nonaka, 1991), verbal knowledge (Corsini, 1987) and declarative knowledge (Kogut and Zander, 1992). It is important to be aware of these various synonyms when attempting to decipher and understand authors' ideas and arguments. Defining objective knowledge is a way of highlighting what tacit knowledge is *not*. In what follows we shall concentrate on what tacit knowledge is, starting with the characteristics of tacit knowledge defined in the resource-based literature.

## Tacit knowledge as defined in resource-based theory

A large majority of authors who write about tacit knowledge refer to Polanyi (1962, 1966, 1976), who is acknowledged to have introduced the concept. Polanyi describes tacit knowledge as follows: 'I shall reconsider human knowledge by starting from the fact that we can know more than we can tell' (Polanyi, 1966, p. 4), or we have a 'power to know more than we can tell' (Polanyi, 1976, p. 336).

One characteristic of tacit knowledge is that it is difficult to write down, to formalise (Nonaka, 1991). People who possess tacit knowledge cannot explain the decision rules that underlie their performance: 'the aim of a skilful performance is achieved by the observance of a set of rules which are not known as such to the person following them' (Polanyi, 1962, p. 49).

Tacit knowledge is also personal knowledge. Sternberg (1994) and Nonaka (1991) argue that it has a cognitive dimension, in the sense that it is scripted. For them, tacit knowledge consists of mental models that individuals follow in certain situations. These are deeply embedded in the individuals and tend to be taken for granted. Ravetz (1971) suggests that tacit knowledge becomes so embedded in the individual that it seems entirely natural. This is one reason why it cannot be expressed and why it is attached to the knower.

Another feature of tacit knowledge is that it is practical (Sternberg, 1994) and describes a process. If, like some authors (Grant, 1991b; Amit and Shoemaker, 1993; Rao, 1994), we were to make a distinction between resources (that is, inputs into the production process) and capabilities (the processes by which the resources are utilised), rather than use the generic term 'resource' (meaning both), it would be appropriate to use the term 'capability' rather than 'resource' when referring to tacit knowledge. In this respect it is similar to know-how (Nonaka, 1991; Kogut and Zander, 1992). Nonaka argues that know-how can be used as a synonym for tacit knowledge because the latter 'consists partly of technical skills – the kind of informal, hard-to-pin down skills captured in the term "know-how"' (Nonaka, 1991, p. 98).

Finally, tacit knowledge is context-specific in that it is 'typically acquired on the job or in the situation where it is used' (Sternberg, 1994, p. 28), or as Nonaka (1991, p. 98) puts it, 'tacit knowledge is . . . deeply rooted in action and in an individual's commitment to a specific context – a craft or a profession, a particular technology or product market, or the activities of a work group or team'.

## Tacit knowledge as a resource

The characteristics described above explain why proponents of the resource-based view are able to argue that tacit knowledge is a source of sustainable competitive advantage: it is unique, imperfectly mobile, imperfectly imitable and non-substitutable. Because it is deeply ingrained in people or organisations, it is taken for granted and is 'difficult for outsiders to imitate or copy' (Sobol and Lei, 1994, p. 171). Tacit knowledge cannot be transposed to other firms because it depends on specific relationships (between colleagues, customers, systems and so on) and because, 'unlike knowledge of a computer code or a chemical formula, it cannot be clearly and completely communicated to someone else through words or other symbols' (Badaracco, 1991, p. 82). Tacitness also generates ambiguity because the organisation is unaware both of the resource and of the actions it undergoes to achieve/create its competitive advantage. In other words the relation between actions and results is causally ambiguous (Reed and DeFillippi, 1990).

While tacit knowledge is clearly a topic of interest in the resource-based literature, it has also been explored in the literature of other disciplines. The following sections review Polanyi's much cited works, Nelson and Winter's evolutionary theory of economic change, some aspects of the organisational culture literature, parts of the occupational and cognitive psychology literature and the teachers' knowledge literature.

## Polanyi on tacit knowledge

In his books *Personal Knowledge* (1962) and *The Tacit Dimension* (1966), Polanyi introduces his ideas on tacit knowledge, which for him is personal knowledge because 'in every act of knowing there enters a passionate contribution of the person knowing what is known'. He goes on, 'I shall take as my clue for this investigation the well-known fact that the aim of a skilful performance is achieved by the observance of a set of rules which are not known as such to the person following them' (Polanyi, 1962, p. 49), and 'I shall reconsider human knowledge by starting from the fact that we can know more than we can tell' (Polanyi, 1966, p. 4). He points out that his 'analysis of knowledge is closely linked to Gestalt psychology' in the sense that Gestalt psychology has shown that we may know something 'by integrating our awareness of its particulars without being able to identify these particulars' (ibid., p. 6).

According to Polanyi, tacit knowledge consists of two elements: subsidiary awareness and focal awareness, which he calls 'the two terms of tacit knowing' (ibid., p. 9). The first of these (subsidiary awareness) is proximal (unconscious) and the second (focal awareness) is distal (conscious). There is a functional relation between the two terms: 'we know the first term only by relying on our awareness of it for attending to the second' (ibid., p. 10). This means that although we have tacit knowledge of the proximal term, we may not be able to say that we have knowledge of it, that is, 'we know more than we can tell' (ibid., p. 4). We know about it only through the distal term and we cannot express it in words. So 'tacit knowledge is a from–to knowing' (Polanyi, 1976, p. 334) – we are aware of something tacitly because our 'attention is elsewhere, on a point of active focal awareness, ahead of it' (Hodgkin, 1992, p. 256). Polanyi (1976, p. 335) indicates that 'the grounds of from–to knowledge [that is, tacit knowledge] may often be unspecifiable'. Hodgkin (1992, p. 256), commenting on Polanyi's work, remarks that 'there can be no doubt that he also included in the concept of tacit knowledge much that would normally be covered by such words as "unconscious" habits that were acquired long ago, for example, and bodily forms and propensities which undoubtedly play a part in tacitly guiding what we do and how we develop'.

To illustrate this Gelwick (1977, p. 64) argues that a focal target can be a problem or a task, and that 'we have some clues of which we are only subsidiarily aware. Sometimes we can stop to pinpoint some of them, but at other times we cannot.' We rely on clues and subsidiary awareness to attend to tasks or problems. The link between the two terms is made by the knower, who links the problem (the focal target) with the clue (the subsidiary term). From the two terms the knower obtains a joint meaning, but does so without being aware of the process.

Finally, it is worth noting that Polanyi argues that tacit knowledge is not 'infallible, it can lead to error as well as to new and truthful insights' (Hodgkin, 1992, p. 255).

## Nelson and Winter's evolutionary theory of economic change

Polanyi's explanation of tacit knowledge was introduced into the strategic management literature, and notably that on the resource-based view of the firm, by Nelson and Winter in *An Evolutionary Theory of Economic Change* (1982). Despite their many differences, the resource-based view of the firm and evolutionary economics share some similarities. In particular they both take an efficiency approach to firms' performance rather than a privileged market position approach, and both emphasise internal factors of the firm as sources of competitive advantage, rather than external factors. Evolutionary economics focuses on routines whereas the resource-based view concentrates on resources in general. However, considering the definition of resource used earlier, it can be stated that the scope of this definition is large enough to encompass Nelson and Winter's 'routines'.

Nelson and Winter (1982, p. 14) define routines as 'all regular and predictable behavioural patterns of firms'. '[R]outines may refer to a repetitive pattern of activity in an entire organisation, to an individual skill, or as an adjective, to the smooth uneventful effectiveness of such an organisational or individual performance' (ibid., p. 97). These 'routines are the skills of an organisation' (ibid., p. 124). They are path-dependent, idiosyncratic and experience-based.

Resources that are seen by resource-based theory as sources of sustainable competitive advantage are those which are rare, non-imitable and non-tradable. This points to knowledge-based resources, and particularly to Nelson and Winter's routines, which is why routines have become central to the resource-based view of the firm. However it is worth noting that the resource-based view focuses on the tacit and slow-to-change aspects of routines that make them difficult to imitate, and not on 'all regular and predictable patterns' (ibid., p. 14). That is, it focuses on routines that are 'ordinarily accomplished without "conscious awareness"' (ibid., p. 125). '[E]ssential coordination information is stored in the routine functioning of the organisation and remembered by doing . . . Much of the knowledge that underlies the effective performance is tacit knowledge of the organisation, not consciously known or articulable by anyone in particular' (ibid., p. 134). It is these aspects of routines that are underpinned by Polanyi – 'the influence of Michael Polanyi is strong in this chapter' (ibid., p. 96) – and that have been much used in the resource-based view of the firm.

Finally it is worth noting that in evolutionary economics routines are not always considered a source of good performance: 'Firms can only do what they have routines for doing. Lacking a routine for a new task, the new task does not really get done' (Langlois, 1995, p. 105). In other words routines may enable an organisation to work but they also limit its ability to change.

## Organisational culture

Organisational culture is an interdisciplinary topic that has been addressed by writers in the fields of organisational behaviour and strategic management. While the organisational culture literature is broad and complex, it is worth considering how culture has been defined and what methodological implications have been drawn as this may inform our exploration of tacit knowledge, in that they can be seen as sharing some characteristics.

### Culture

The purpose of this and the following subsection is not to review the organisational culture literature in general as the concept is too multifaceted and intricate to be dealt with in a few lines. As Ogbonna (1993, p. 42) writes, 'there is no consensus on the definition of culture. . . . There are as many definitions of culture as there are experts on the subject.' We shall concentrate on Schein's view of what organisational culture involves as this has direct relevance for the current topic.

In *Organizational culture and leadership*, Schein defines culture as 'the deeper level of basic assumptions and beliefs that are shared by members of an organisation, that operate unconsciously, and that define in a basic "taken-for-granted" fashion an organisation's view of itself and its environment' (Schein, 1985, p. 6). He has also defined culture as 'the pattern of basic assumptions that a given group has invented, discovered, or developed in learning to cope with its problems of external adaptation and internal integration and that have worked well enough to be considered valid, and, therefore, to be taught to new members as the correct way to perceive, think and feel in relation to these problems'

(Schein, 1992, p. 237). The essence of culture is 'the pattern of assumptions that underlie what people value and do' (Schein, 1985, p. 112).

For Schein, culture is a three-level process; the first level (the more visible) being the artifacts and creation level, that is, behavioural patterns; the second being the values, that is, the reasons behind the behaviours; and the third (the invisible one) being the taken-for-granted assumptions. According to Schein it is the third level that forms the core of an organisation's culture. These taken-for-granted assumptions 'exist outside ordinary awareness and are for the most part inaccessible to consciousness' (Hatch, 1997, p. 210), 'are the aspects of organisational life which people find difficult to identify and explain' (Johnson and Scholes, 1997, p. 217), and constitute what Johnson (1988) calls 'the organisational paradigm'.

Schein suggests that values (the second level) can progressively be transformed into basic assumptions. This occurs if the value 'continues to work, thus implying that it is in some larger sense "correct" and must reflect an accurate picture of reality' (Schein, 1985, p. 16), and 'as the values begin to be taken for granted, they gradually become beliefs and assumptions and drop out of consciousness, just as habits become unconscious and automatic' (ibid., p. 17). The basic assumptions then tend to become 'nonconfrontable and nondebatable', and organisational members 'would find behaviour based on any other premise [than these assumptions] inconceivable' (ibid., p. 18).

According to Schein, 'basic assumptions are hard to locate' (ibid., p. 20) and he has 'found no reliable, quick way to identify cultural assumptions' (ibid., p. 135). He suggests that both 'clinical' interviews and anthropologists' methods of data gathering should be employed, and that triangulating data and establishing a dialogue between insiders and outsiders are necessary. He also insists that questionnaires and formalised tests are of no use when looking at cultural assumptions.

Similarly to Schein, Johnson (1988, p. 85) writes that the paradigm 'may be difficult to surface as a coherent statement', and that the paradigm can be understood not just as a set of beliefs and assumptions, but also as an element 'preserved and legitimised in a "cultural web" of organisational action in terms of myths, rituals, symbols, control systems and formal and informal power structures which support and provide relevance to core beliefs'. In other words basic assumptions are not removed from organisational action but lie within the 'cultural web which bonds them to the day-to-day action of organisational life' (Johnson and Scholes, 1993, p. 60). This implies that even if one cannot find direct ways of studying the paradigm, one can do so indirectly by looking at each of the other elements of the culture (including how they relate to and overlap each other). This indirect method of studying taken-for-granted assumptions can be relevant to the study of tacit knowledge, especially as tacit knowledge can be regarded as an element of organisational culture, or as Sternberg (1995, p. 324) writes, 'organisational cultures are vast repositories of tacit knowledge'.

Finally, because the core of organisational culture is taken for granted and hardly ever questioned, it is very difficult to change and may hinder organisational change and innovation – it may cause organisations to fail to adapt to environmental changes as it contributes to organisational inertia.

### Theories in use

What Schein (1985) calls basic assumptions and Johnson (1988) refers to as the paradigm are similar to Argyris and Schön's (1974) 'theories-in-use' and Schön's (1987) 'knowing in action'. Theories-in-use are 'if–then' propositions individuals use without necessarily being able to describe them (Schön, 1983) – they are skilful performances that 'we are characteristically unable to make verbally explicit' (Schön, 1987, p. 25). 'Knowing in action is embedded in the socially and institutionally structured context', it goes 'beyond available rules, facts, theories and operations' (Schön, 1994, p. 243). Theories-in-use can be in opposition to the so-called 'espoused theories', the if–then propositions that individuals think lie behind their actions. Individuals are often unaware that their theories-in-use are not in accordance with their espoused strategies. This is due to the fact that their behaviour has been learned in their early life, 'hence the behaviour is highly skilled. All skilful activity is so automatic that it is taken for granted. It becomes tacit' (Argyris, 1996, p. 4). Theories-in-use can be found at both the collective and the individual level and can be sources of both competence and incompetence. They can be both functional and dysfunctional.

### Occupational psychology

This section and that which follows highlight the fact that tacit knowledge is an interdisciplinary topic, and that viewing it from only one perspective does not provide a sufficiently complete picture.

Sternberg and Wagner view tacit knowledge as a measure of practical intelligence that predicts job success in a way that goes beyond IQ. Their work starts with the premise that beyond a necessary IQ level, 'IQ and scores from other ability and achievement tests make little difference to managerial success' (Wagner and Sternberg, 1991, p. 333), as IQ is only a measure of academic intelligence and not of practical intelligence. What matters in real-world pursuits is tacit knowledge.

Wagner and Sternberg define tacit knowledge as 'work-related know-how that is acquired in the absence of direct instruction' (ibid., p. 333). It is 'typically acquired on the job or in the situation where it is used' (Sternberg, 1994, p. 28). It cannot be used outside its context of use, and it is 'acquired as people interact with a real environment . . . rarely in artificial situations whether in the classroom or otherwise' (Sternberg, 1995, p. 323). Tacit knowledge is practical rather than academic, it is 'intimately related to action' (Sternberg *et al.*, 1995, p. 916), it is informal rather than formal and it is usually not directly taught. Furthermore it is 'usually is not openly expressed or stated' (Wagner and Sternberg, 1986, p. 51), and 'people generally don't know the tacit knowledge they have and use' (Sternberg, 1995, p. 324). According to Sternberg (1994, pp. 30, 31), 'tacit knowledge takes the form of condition – action sequences', 'it is a knowledge about what to do and when', and it 'is part of a script or schema people follow in certain situations'. Wagner and Sternberg argue that there are different categories of tacit knowledge in 'real-world settings': tacit knowledge about oneself, tacit knowledge about others and tacit knowledge about tasks. Such knowledge can be either local or global (that is involving short-term or long-term actions).

Wagner and Sternberg acknowledge that the concept of tacit knowledge was first introduced by Polanyi and state that in many respects their definition matches his. However they are not as strict as he is about the meaning of tacit. Indeed they note that 'by our use of the word tacit we do not wish to imply that such knowledge is completely inaccessible to conscious awareness, unspeakable, or even untouchable, but merely that it is usually not taught directly to most of us' (Wagner and Sternberg, 1986, p. 54). Sternberg (1995, p. 324) also remarks that 'tacit knowledge is "conservative", it represents the way things are, which may or not be the ways things should be', and that, echoing Nelson and Winter (1982), 'tacit knowledge can be wrong' (Sternberg, 1994, p. 29). It can be a source of success or of failure.

## Cognitive psychology

When looking at tacit knowledge it is important to consider the cognitive psychology literature because, as emphasised by Eysenck and Keane (1994, p. 293), 'knowledge is one of the oldest and most researched areas in cognitive psychology'. The area covered by the cognitive psychology literature is particularly broad and the following subsections consider just a few of the categories that deal with knowledge. It should be noted that these categories are not discrete but rather overlap each other.

## Knowledge and memory

According to Reed (1996, p. 5), memory is 'the storage and recovery of information'. Broadly, humans have two types of memory storage: short term and long term (Waugh and Norman, 1965). Short-term memory is limited in both capacity and duration, whereas long-term memory has neither of these limitations. This distinction is fairly basic and others have argued that the memory system is far more complex. In particular there have been several claims that long-term memory is not a single, unitary system. For instance Tulving (1985) proposes that long-term memory is divided into episodic memory, memory of personal experiences and semantic memory, or memory of general knowledge. It has also been proposed that long-term memory is composed of declarative memory, memory for facts and procedural memory, 'memory for actions, skills and operations' – (Reed, 1996, p. 140), and similarly that declarative and procedural knowledge is stored in the long-term memory. Declarative knowledge 'refers to knowledge of facts, such as knowledge of concepts and knowledge of individuals and events in the world' (Stevenson, 1993, p. 26). While 'declarative knowledge is knowledge that can be reported and is not tied to the situation in which it can be used' (Eysenck and Keane, 1994, p. 397), procedural knowledge 'refers to knowledge about how to do things' (Stevenson, 1993, p. 26) and 'to the ability to perform skilled actions . . . without the involvement of conscious recollection' (Eysenck and Keane, 1994, p. 192). Procedural memory is associated with 'anoetic (nonknowing) consciousness' (Tulving, 1985, p. 388), and 'procedural knowledge is applied automatically, often cannot be reported, and is specifically tuned to be applied in specific situations' (Eysenck and Keane, 1994, p. 397). Declarative knowledge corresponds to Ryle's (1949) 'knowing that' and procedural knowledge corresponds to 'knowing how'.

## Expert knowledge

Experts differ from novices in task performance relative to their field of expertise (Chi *et al.*, 1981), and notably in the amount of knowledge they have and the organisation of this knowledge, rather than in their cognitive abilities. For example studies of chess masters and physicists have shown that unlike experts, novices cannot link problem situations to principles and that they use domain-independent knowledge rather than domain-specific knowledge. The main methods of research are observing experts perform their tasks, interviews and protocol analysis (thinking aloud).

There is considerable agreement in the 'expert knowledge' literature (knowledge engineering, knowledge acquisition, expertise) that much of an expert's knowledge is tacit (Berry, 1987; Hardiman, 1987). For instance Ford and Wood (1992, p. 3) point out the 'common observation that much of an expert's problem solving occurs "automatically", without conscious reflection or even conscious awareness', and Masters (1992, p. 344) argues that 'the characteristics of expertise most definitely involve functioning of an automatic, effortless, implicit nature'. Authors also agree that at present there is no satisfactory way of eliciting experts' implicit knowledge (Berry, 1987) and that codifying knowledge held by an expert is an extremely difficult process (Clarke, 1987).

Rather than employing the terms 'declarative knowledge' and 'procedural knowledge', researchers on expert knowledge tend to use 'explicit knowledge' and 'implicit knowledge'. Their definitions are similar if not identical. For example Masters (1992, p. 343) defines explicit knowledge as that which is 'made up of facts and rules of which we are specifically aware and therefore able to articulate', and Berry (1994, p. 756) defines it as knowledge that is 'accessible to consciousness and that can be communicated or demonstrated on demand'. Similarly Masters (1992, p. 343) defines implicit knowledge as being 'made up of that which we "know", yet are not aware of and thus cannot articulate', while Berry (1994, p. 756) defines it as knowledge that is 'less accessible to consciousness and cannot easily be communicated or demonstrated on demand'.

The following findings on what characterises expert knowledge explain why the knowledge held by experts is believed to be largely implicit:

- '[E]xpert knowledge is acquired slowly over a long period of time' (Hardiman, 1987, p. 6).
- '[T]he knowledge of an expert is highly proceduralised' (Glaser, 1985, p. 8).
- '[E]xperts are goal driven' (ibid., p. 9).
- '[E]xperts display specific domain intelligence' (ibid.), 'expertise remains at the mercy of its context' (Agnew *et al.*, 1994, p. 68), and 'the development of expertise is subject to tasks, demands and the "social structure" of the job situation' (Glaser, 1985, p. 9).
- '[M]any experts are unable to express their knowledge in clear, propositional form' (Hardiman, 1987, p. 7), and it is difficult for experts to report on their knowledge (Ford and Wood, 1992).

As people become more skilled at performing certain tasks they become less aware of how they perform these tasks. Therefore it is 'difficult for experts to articulate their problem-solving strategies effectively as they are themselves not fully cognizant of the steps involved' (Agarwal and Tanniru, 1990, p. 124). This is what Johnson (1983) calls 'paradox of expertise', which leads us back to the issue of memory in that this paradox is said to exist because 'the limited storage capacity of attentional memory hinders the ability of the expert to recall situations in the past that form an essential part of his/her expertise' (Agarwal and Tanniru, 1990, p. 124). This brings us to the question of how experts acquire their knowledge.

### Expert knowledge and skill acquisition

Berry (1987, p. 145) distinguishes between two types of implicit knowledge: knowledge that 'was once represented explicitly or declaratively', and implicit knowledge, 'which arises as a result of an implicit learning process and has never been explicitly represented'. The former type is described by Anderson (1983) in his theory of skill acquisition. He suggests that novices solve problems by using their declarative knowledge (that is, they use domain-free strategies and deliberate and conscious processes to solve problems), while experts use procedural knowledge (they use domain-specific rules and specific actions that can be retrieved automatically). According to Anderson, experts have turned their declarative knowledge into procedural knowledge and have fine-tuned this procedural knowledge through practice. This type of skill acquisition is the one most described in the expert knowledge literature.

Similarly to Anderson, Johnson (1983) proposes a three-stage model of expert knowledge acquisition: the cognition stage, where individuals learn what to do by means of instruction or observation; the associative phase of learning stage, where the actions learned in the first stage are practised until they become smooth and accurate; and the automaticity of action stage, in which practised actions can now be done without thinking. The results of this last phase 'are usually not available to conscious awareness', and hence are 'the kind of knowledge Michael Polanyi referred to as tacit' (Johnson, 1983, p. 79). This is due to the process of cognitive adaptation: because of the lack of short-term memory people have 'to convert much of [their] knowledge into forms for storage that are unavailable to conscious awareness' (ibid., p. 80).

The second type of implicit knowledge is similar to the form of learning described by Reber (1989) in his study of synthetic grammar learning. This knowledge is learned through experience and is 'acquired independently of conscious attempts to do so' (ibid., p. 219).

## Intuition

For Shirley and Langan-Fox (1996, p. 573) the 'concepts of intuition and tacit knowledge appear to be very similar'. They define intuition, following Vaughan (1979, p. 46), as 'knowing without being able to explain how we know' and add that 'research needs to be conducted to refine the definitions of these terms and to investigate whether and how they differ from one another' (Shirley and Langan-Fox, 1996, p. 573).

## Teachers' knowledge

This penultimate section of the chapter – which has set out to demonstrate that the consideration of tacit knowledge has extended beyond the confines of the resource-based view of the firm – outlines how tacit knowledge has been treated in the literature on teachers and their knowledge. The review will not be exhaustive, but it should help to provide a more rounded view of tacit knowledge.

Teachers' knowledge, and particularly teachers' practical knowledge, 'has become a central concern of curriculum scholars' (Elbaz, 1991, p. 1). Practical knowledge is useful to consider when attempting to understand what tacit knowledge is about. One characteristic of teachers' practical knowledge is that it can be considered as 'knowledge as process' rather than 'knowledge as product' (Elbaz, 1983). It 'is a knowledge in process, which emerges in the flow of practical activity [and], is directed towards ends' (Johnson, 1989, p. 363). Such knowledge also 'has a social orientation': it is 'shaped by social constraints' and 'is held in the context of the particular experiences through which it was acquired and is experientially oriented in that it reflects and gives shape to the knower's experience' (Elbaz, 1983, pp. 101, 102).

Elbaz writes that teachers' practical knowledge encompasses their first-hand experience of students, their classroom skills, their knowledge of the social structure of the school, and their knowledge of the subject matter of the school and of other subjects such as child development. She adds that this knowledge is individual and hence attuned to the teacher's unique purposes. Johnson's (1989) definition is much broader. Indeed for him teachers' practical knowledge 'would include the entire way in which they have a structured world that they can make some sense of, and in which they can function with varying degrees of success' (ibid., p. 363). Similarly to those in other fields who are interested in knowledge, authors working on the issue of teachers' knowledge have acknowledged that such research is complex (Yinger, 1986), and have argued that one way of researching teachers' practical knowledge is to use qualitative methods.

## Summary of the tacit knowledge literature

Each of the fields explored above can help us to achieve a better understanding of the nature of tacit knowledge. Despite some differences between these perspectives they have a number of commonalties (see also Figure 2.1). Most refer to Polanyi, and argue that tacit knowledge:

- Is taken for granted.
- Is action-based.
- Is context-specific.
- Is experience-based.
- Is difficult to express.
- Generates causal ambiguity.
- Can be both valuable and hindering.
- Is awkward to research.

The issues linked to tacit knowledge are not limited to its complexity, ambiguity and terminology, and one could also ask whether it is embedded only in specific individuals or whether it can also be embedded in an organisation. Theoretically both are supported. The following chapter reviews some of the literature on this issue.

**POLANYI**
- References: Polanyi (1962, 1966)
- Terminology: tacit knowledge
- Individual knowledge
- Valuable and hindering
- Difficult to express
- Generates causal ambiguity
- Context-specific

**RESOURCE-BASED THEORY**
- References: Nonaka (1991), Sobol and Lei (1994)
- Terminology: tacit / implicit knowledge
- Based on Polanyi
- Individual and group knowledge
- Source of sustainable competitive advantage
- Difficult to express
- Generates causal ambiguity
- Practical
- Context-specific

**EVOLUTIONARY ECONOMICS**
- Reference: Nelson and Winter (1982)
- Terminology: tacit routines
- Based on Polanyi
- Group knowledge
- Functional and dysfunctional
- Difficult to express
- Generates causal ambiguity
- Practical
- Context-specific

**COGNITIVE PSYCHOLOGY**

*Memory*
- References: Reed (1996), Eysenck and Keane (1994)
- Terminology: procedural memory
- Individuals' memory
- Action-based
- No conscious recollection
- Context-specific

*Expertise*
- References: Berry (1987), Masters (1982)
- Terminology: expert / tacit knowledge
- Based on Polanyi
- Individual knowledge
- Practical
- Difficult to express
- Context-specific
- Valuable

*Skill acquisition*
- References: Anderson (1983), Johnson (1983)
- Terminology: procedural knowledge
- Individual knowledge
- Practical
- Difficult to express
- Context-specific

**TACIT KNOWLEDGE**

**OCCUPATIONAL PSYCHOLOGY**
- References: Wagner and Sternberg (1985, 1986)
- Terminology: tacit knowledge
- Based on Polanyi
- Individual knowledge
- Source of success and failure
- Difficult to express (but can be)
- Generates causal ambiguity
- Practical
- Context-specific

**TEACHERS' KNOWLEDGE**
- References: Elbaz (1983, 1991), Johnson (1989)
- Terminology: practical knowledge
- Individual knowledge
- Valuable
- Practical
- Context-specific

**ORGANISATIONAL CULTURE**

*Culture*
- References: Schein (1985), Johnson (1988)
- Terminology: basic assumptions/paradigm
- Group level
- Functional and dysfunctional
- Taken-for-granted
- Action-based
- Context-specific

*Theories-in-use*
- References: Argyris and Schön (1974), Schön (1987)
- Terminology: Theories-in use/knowing in action
- Individual and group level
- Functional and dysfunctional
- Taken-for-granted
- Action-based
- Context-specific

*Figure 2.1* Summary of the tacit knowledge literature

# 3
# Organisational Knowledge

While the works reviewed in Chapter 2 can help us to comprehend the concept of tacit knowledge more fully, the majority deal with tacit knowledge at the individual level. This is important, but what may be more interesting is tacit knowledge at the organisational level – that is, tacit knowledge as a source of sustainable competitive advantage. Individual tacit knowledge can disappear when the individuals who hold the knowledge leave the organisation. It is easily transferable, 'moving with the person, [and thus] giving rise to potential problems of retention' (Lam, 2000, p. 491). This makes the organisation vulnerable to the loss of tacit knowledge to competitors. Furthermore individuals 'die off and their tacit knowledge dies with them' (Boisot, 1998, p. 38). All this means that competitive advantage based on individual tacit knowledge is inherently precarious. This does not apply so strongly to organisational tacit knowledge as 'such knowledge cannot be moved into an organisation without the transfer of clusters of individuals with established patterns of working together' (Teece, 2000, p. 36).

What organisational knowledge relates to is a matter of debate. The term 'knowledge' raises the question of whether organisational knowledge exists, in contrast to individual knowledge, and 'whether organisations as entities can do anything in their own rights' (Hedberg, 1981, p. 3). In the following sections the three main positions on the question are outlined.

## The 'individualistic or reductionist' thesis

Advocates of this thesis argue that only individuals can perceive, think, decide and act on their own. For them, groups are nothing more than the sum of the actions of each group member taken individually. In other words, groups are 'solely the products of individual behaviour and individual motives' (Asch, 1952, p. 242). Among the supporters of this proposition are Adler and Shenbar (1990), who declare that 'the organisation "knows" only what its employees and managers have learned' (ibid., p. 28), and March and Olsen (1976), who assert that 'it is individuals who act and who learn from acting; organisations are the stages where acting takes place' (ibid., p. 3). This idea is not recent. Indeed in the early 1960s Cyert and March (1963, p. 26) wrote that 'people (*i.e.* individuals) have goals, collectivities of people do not'. Hence for individualists 'organisations are merely constructs' (Hedberg, 1981, p. 6). The proposition that only individuals can decide or act clearly dismisses the notion that organisations can learn or possess knowledge in any meaningful sense. This standpoint is rejected by the so-called 'group mind' thesis.

## The 'group mind' thesis

This thesis is the polar opposite of the preceding one. According to Asch (1952, p. 242), the thesis:

> begins with the observation that when men live and act in groups there arise forces and phenomena that follow laws of their own and which cannot be described in terms of the properties of individuals composing them. ... These are processes over and above those which we find in individuals taken singly and which can no longer be traced back to them. They have laws of their own, different from the characteristics of individuals and not reducible to them.

The main defender of this position was Durkheim, who suggested that individual minds 'forming groups . . . give birth to a being . . . constituting a psychic individuality of a new sort' (Durkheim, 1938, p. 103). This theory is rarely supported in the management literature, where the most widely accepted concept is that described as the 'individual–group relation' thesis.

## The 'individual–group relation' thesis

This thesis proposes that the individualistic and the group mind theses are too extreme. The basis of the thesis is that a group 'does not reside in the individuals taken separately though each individual contributes to it; nor does it reside outside them; it is present in the interrelations between the activities of individuals' (Asch, 1952, p. 252), and that 'although learning is based on individuals in the workforce, firms can learn *in toto*' (Dodgson, 1993, p. 377). This means that 'the output [and notably knowledge] is yielded by a team . . . and it is not a sum of separable outputs of each of its members' (Alchian and Demsetz, 1972, p. 779).

This view of organisations as social systems (Gharajedaghi and Ackoff, 1994) – that is, that an organisation is more than the sum of its independent parts (including the environment) and that what one part does influences the others – is shared by a large number of authors working on a range of topics, including organisational interpretation (Daft and Weick, 1984), the collective mind (Weick and Roberts, 1993) and organisational memory (Walsh and Ungson, 1991). They all suggest that an organisation has '"something more" . . . beyond the sum of the parts that make the organisation' (Jelinek, 1979, p. xii), or to quote Weick and Roberts (1993, p. 360), 'a collective mind is distinct from an individual mind because it inheres in the pattern of interrelated activities among many people'. Kogut and Zander's (1992) proposition that organisational knowledge rests on the organising of human resources, that it is embedded in enduring individual relationships, and Lyles and Schwenk's (1992) suggestion that organisational knowledge structures are built out of social processes, share the same core notion. From this it can be deduced that 'firms . . . are in essence, vast, complex repositories of knowledge' (Badaracco, 1991, p. 80). Hence while 'individuals come and go . . . organisations preserve knowledge, behaviours, mental maps, norms, and values over time' (Daft and Weick, 1984, p. 285). Therefore organisational knowledge exists. Furthermore it is different from individual knowledge, even if it is linked to it.

### Organisational knowledge and organisational routines

For proponents of this position an organisation is more than the sum of its parts, and what one part does influences the others. The general argument is that it is *routines* that give 'organisations consistent properties regardless of their temporary memberships' (Hedberg, 1981, p. 20). In other words, organisational knowledge is embedded in a firm's routines. This view is reflected in Badaracco's claim that 'organisations . . . do not know what they know in the same ways as individuals, but knowledge and capabilities do reside in the interstices of their routines, practices, culture, and working relationships' (Badaracco, 1991, p. 90). This is supported by Sobol and Lei (1994, p. 171), who assert that it is 'routines that become highly firm-specific that lay the foundation for building new sources of insights, experiences and competences'. This assertion can be seen as being largely based on Nelson and Winter's (1982) view. Indeed according to them it is the establishment of routines that operationalise organisations' memories and knowledge bases, and knowledge borne of specialised knowledge becomes embedded in organisational routines. They suggest that organisations remember through informal and formal routines. They 'remember by doing'. Nelson and Winter's position is unambiguous, and they stress that 'to view organisational memory as reducible to individual memories is to overlook, or undervalue, the linking of those individual memories by shared experiences in the past, experiences that have established the extremely detailed and specified communication system that underlies routine performance' (ibid., p. 105).

This suggests that organisational knowledge may be tacit, an idea supported by authors such as Grant (1991b) and Wright (1994). Grant (1991b, p. 110) specifies that 'organisational routines involve a large component of tacit knowledge which implies limits on the extent to which organisation's capabilities can be articulated'. These types of routine are firm-specific, taken-for-granted, path-dependent, complex and so on, and therefore are difficult to imitate. They can be seen as a possible resource in the resource-based view of the firm (valuable, rare, imperfectly mobile, imitable and substitutable). The concept of organisational routines being a repository for organisational knowledge implies that when dealing with tacit knowledge at the organisational level one is actually dealing with the tacit *routines* of the organisation, the tacit *ways of doing things*, the tacit *activities* in which people in the organisation are involved.

# Part II

# Research Terminology

# 4
## Working Definitions

In Part I the core propositions of the resource-based view of the firm were described, and it was stated that tacit knowledge is widely argued to be a source of sustainable competitive advantage. However this discussion was theoretical as tacit knowledge has so far resisted operationalisation. Indeed, 'despite widespread agreement among researchers that intangible resources underlie performance differences among organisations, little evidence [of this] exists in the literature' (Rao, 1994, p. 29). Therefore if the concept is to be developed and operationalised it needs to be defined more precisely.

As there is no accepted measure of sustainable competitive advantage (Brumagin, 1994), and as an interpretive perspective was adopted in my research, like other authors (for example Miller, 1988) I have opted to use a subjective measure of firm performance. I believe that using the perceptions of knowledgeable key participants is a valid approach, and it can be argued that top team members should be at least as knowledgeable about their organisation's success as anybody else, and arguably they should be more knowledgeable. Hence I have decided that for the purposes of this study any organisation whose top managers perceive that their organisation is successful and has been so for a while, should be considered as displaying sustainable competitive advantage. In other words I have decided to opt for a proxy 'measure' of sustainable competitive advantage in the form of top managers' judgement of their firm's success and their accounts of the firm's success.

When reading the literature on tacit knowledge it soon becomes clear that there are variations in the terms used, and therefore comparing and developing of ideas can be problematic. In this chapter it is argued that the term 'tacit skills' is preferable to 'tacit knowledge' when dealing with individual tacit knowledge, and that 'tacit routines' is preferable when dealing with tacit organisational knowledge. This provides clarity and emphasises the argument put forward by the resource-based view of the firm that easily traded and imitable resources are unlikely to be sources of advantage. What is most likely to make a difference is *action in context*, the *activities that people perform* – that is, how various resources in the most general sense are utilised to enable the firm to operate more efficiently and effectively than its competitors.

## Tacit skills

There are numerous synonyms for tacit knowledge. For instance Nelson and Winter (1982) state that tacit knowing is what is ordinarily called a skill. 'Know-how' is another alternative (Corsini, 1987; Kogut and Zander, 1992), and Kogut and Zander (1992) believe that 'recipe' is comparable to know-how, and hence to tacit knowledge. Tacit knowledge is also referred to as unarticulated and implicit (Spender, 1994), uncodifiable (Hu, 1995) and procedural (as opposed to declarative) knowledge. Finally, for Polanyi (1976) tacit knowledge is what he calls 'from – to' (or 'from – at') knowing.

Apart from the confusion caused by the use of these multiple expressions, employing the word 'knowledge' – be it qualified with tacit or implicit, or procedural or unarticulated – may be inappropriate when dealing with tacit knowledge. There are two reasons for this assertion. First, the observation that 'when we hear the term "knowledge", we tend to think "science" and "objectivity"' (Spender, 1993, p. 246) means that tacit knowledge is a difficult concept to come to terms with because 'tacit' implies subjectivity and 'knowledge' implies some degree of objectivity. Hence there is a mismatch and the terms are difficult to reconcile, so one needs to think beyond the first meaning of knowledge. Second, as we saw in Chapter 2, when looking at the definitions of tacit knowledge the word 'doing' (or other equivalents) commonly occurs. Thus there are definitions that state that tacit knowledge is practical (Sternberg, 1994), that it is similar to know-how, that it is about how to do something rather than knowing what to do (Kogut and Zander, 1992), that it is a competence (Badaracco, 1991), that it is partly composed of technical skills (Nonaka, 1991) and that it is embedded in work practices (Spender, 1994). Therefore when dealing with individual tacit knowledge in an organisational setting the expression 'tacit knowledge' is best replaced by 'tacit skills', with skills implying 'doing'. Drawing a distinction between tacit skills and tacit knowledge helps make explicit the idea that tacit knowledge is not about 'knowing about', knowing in the abstract, but that it is about *action*, about *doing*. Tacit knowledge is practical.

## Tacit routines

As explained earlier, the main interest in strategy resides in organisational tacit knowledge rather than individual tacit knowledge because individual 'knowledge can, of course, be more readily bought and sold' (Teece, 2000, p. 36) and hence may not be a source of sustainable competitive advantage. However when tacit knowledge is being discussed, very often the distinction between individual tacit knowledge and organisational tacit knowledge either is not made or is blurred. Employing the term tacit routines rather than organisational tacit knowledge should reduce this confusion.

Before proceeding further it will be helpful to clarify what is meant here by routines as a variety of definitions of routines and their properties exist in the literature. A few of these are shown in the Table 4.1. As discussed earlier, tacit routines can be seen as synonymous with organisational tacit

*Table 4.1*  Authors' definitions of organisational routines and their properties

| | |
|---|---|
| Nelson and Winter (1982) | 'Routines may refer to a repetitive pattern of activity in an entire organisation, to an individual skill, or as an adjective to the smooth uneventful effectiveness of such an organisational individual performance' (p. 92). |
| | Routines are 'our general term for all regular and predictable behavioural patterns of firms' (p. 14). |
| | 'Routines are essentially automatic, executed without explicit deliberation or choice' (Pentland and Rueter, 1994, p. 488, commenting on Nelson and Winter). |
| Levitt and March (1988) | 'The generic term "routines" includes the forms, rules, procedures, conventions, strategies, and technologies around which organisations are constructed and through which they operate. It also includes the structure of beliefs, frameworks, paradigms, codes, cultures and knowledge that buttress, elaborate, and contradict the formal routines' (p. 320). |
| Pentland and Rueter (1994) | Routines 'can be seen as a set of possible patterns that need not be fixed and automatic' (p. 485). This definition is midway between Nelson and Winter's (1982) view and the sociologist view (Giddens, 1984) that routines are effortful accomplishments and are not automatic. |
| | 'Routines are difficult to study because they are essentially patterns of social actions' (p. 484). |

*Table 4.1   Continued*

| | |
|---|---|
| Grant (1996) | An organisational routine is 'a mechanism for co-ordination which is not dependent upon the need for communication of knowledge in explicit form' (p. 379). |
| Johnson and Scholes (1997) | Routines are 'the ways we do things around here'. |
| Cohen and Bacdayan (1994) | Organisational routines are 'multi-actor, interlocking [and] reciprocally triggered sequences of actions' (p. 554). They are 'frequently repeated action sequences' (p. 554). |
| | Routines 'designate established patterns of organisational action and we distinguish routines from "standard operating procedures" which are more explicitly formulated and have normative standing' (p. 555). |
| | 'Individuals store their components of organisational routines in their procedural memory' (p. 554). |
| | Routines 'are hard to observe, analyse and describe' (p. 554). |
| | Routines are stored in the procedural memory, that is, 'memory for how things are done that is relatively automatic and inarticulate and . . . encompasses both cognitive and motor activities' (p. 554). |
| | Routines are emergent and history dependent. |
| | 'The parts of routines held by individuals is often partially inarticulate' (p. 556). |
| Spender (1996) | Routines are about praxis. |
| Dodgson (1993) | 'The concept of routine implies organisational action' (p. 383). |
| Ashford and Fried (1988) | Routines are sustained by the cognitive structures of individual organisational members. |
| Teece (1990) | 'Routines cannot be codified' (p. 67) They provide the underpinnings for a firm's distinctive performance. |
| Spender and Baumard (1995) | Organisational routines are partly tacit. |
| Miller (1996) | 'Routines can create inertia, tunnel vision, rigidity' (p. 495). |

knowledge as both phenomena are difficult to verbalise; they are about doing, and they are context-specific. Tacit routines are not standard operating procedures; they are not organisational routines that are specified by procedures or codified in a rule book; they are not organisational policies or specified norms of behaviour – that is, prescribed ways of doing business – but relate to real ways of doing business. Tacit routines are ways of doing things in the organisation, things that people do that are not explicitly articulated and are not readily verbalised. They are about action, about doing. They are activities that people perform. *So when dealing with organisational tacit knowledge in this book the terms tacit routines and tacit activities (or tacit ways of doing things) will be used interchangeably.*

## Tacit routines and tacit skills

It was argued above that individual tacit knowledge should be considered as tacit skills and organisational tacit knowledge as tacit routines. Tacit skills and tacit routines are similar in most aspects: they are context-specific, difficult to articulate and actionbased. But whereas the outcome of a tacit skill can be attributed to a single individual, the outcome of a tacit activity cannot be clearly attributed to one person, and no single individual can know everything about how that outcome was reached.

## Defining 'tacit'

A review of the literature (Polanyi, 1962; Reber 1989; Nonaka, 1991; Spender 1996) shows that there are varying degrees of tacitness (Figure 4.1).

At the two extremes in Figure 4.1 are explicit routines (routines that are easily communicated, codified and shared) and deeply ingrained tacit routines. In between these two there are two other degrees of tacitness (B and C), which are based on the definitions of tacit knowledge presented in Chapter 2, notably those by Wagner and Sternberg (1986) (see the section on occupational psychology in Chapter 2). The tacit routines in C cannot be expressed through the normal use of words but may be articulated in other ways, for example through metaphors or story telling. The tacit routines in B are unarticulated but could be readily articulated if employees were simply asked 'How do you do that?' These routines are tacit only because nobody has ever asked the right question – people have never asked themselves what they are doing and nobody else has asked them either.

The lack of empirical work on the subject shows that research on tacit routines is still at the exploratory stage so operationalising the most tacit

| D | Deeply ingrained tacit routines |
| C | Tacit routines that can only be imperfectly articulated |
| B | Tacit routines that can be articulated |
| A | Explicit routines |

*Figure 4.1*   Degrees of tacitness (adapted from Ambrosini and Bowman (2001a))

of tacit routines is unlikely to be a realistic endeavour, especially in the field of strategic management. However operationalising tacit routines that have not yet been articulated but could be so if the right question was asked or if they were expressed through means other than formal words may be achievable and would give researchers and managers a better chance of understanding how their firms achieve success. Hence in my research I decided to concentrate on tacit routines B and C.

# Part III

# The Research Project: Methodology

# 5
# Researching Tacit Activities: Methodology Suggested by the Literature

## Tacit knowledge as a valuable resource

Before turning to the key questions of the research project I would like to point out that writers on the resource-based view of the firm tend to take a one-sided view of tacit knowledge: they mainly concentrate on its positive aspects (Leonard-Barton, 1992, is a notable exception) and assume that tacit knowledge is valuable and a source of competitive advantage. However tacit knowledge can also be source of dysfunctionality – it can become a 'competency trap' (Levitt and March, 1988), which can lead to 'core rigidities' (Leonard-Barton, 1992). Embedded routines that have worked in the past can eventually lead to dysfunctionality. They may block adaptation to changes in the environment, hinder innovation and lead to the continuation of inferior work practices.

In my project, though following the resource-based view of the firm's argument, I concentrated on *valuable* routines as the purpose of the study was to consider whether tacit organisational knowledge – that is, tacit activities – played a crucial part in firms' success. As discussed earlier, it is widely acknowledged that tacit knowledge can be a source of sustainable advantage. However there is little empirical work to support this proposition and this gave me my starting point: I wanted to examine whether the proposition could be empirically substantiated. Based on the elaboration of the concepts of tacit knowledge and sustainable competitive advantage presented in the previous chapters, my working research questions were as follows:

- Are tacit activities perceived by managers to be a component of their firm's success?

- What are the implications of tacit routines for the management of organisational success and for strategic management?

## Philosophical perspectives

In the field of social science, broadly speaking, there are two main schools, each with a different view of research: positivism and interpretive social science (Silverman, 1993). Briefly, the key idea of positivism is that the social world exists externally and is objective (Easterby-Smith *et al.*, 1992), whereas the underpinning idea of interpretive social research is that reality is socially constructed and subjective. This means that in the positivist school the researcher is independent and tends to use large samples, and that in the interpretive school the researcher tends to be closely involved and there is a focus for small samples (ibid.) The present research is based on the interpretive or constructivist view. The next section explains why.

Before explaining why I decided to adopt an interpretive perspective I shall briefly explain why I rejected the positivist framework. The decision was based on the defining features of tacit knowledge. In previous chapters it was explained that tacit knowledge depends on the knower and is context-specific. The first feature is obviously not in line with the Cartesian split between subject and object, knower and known, and the second implies that the same tacit knowledge is not to be found in a wide range of firms, that is, it is not generalisable. This suggests that studying tacit knowledge within the positivist framework would not be suitable.

I believe that the world is socially constructed, that is, 'people are constantly involved in interpreting their world' (Blaikie, 1993, p. 36). However, while people construct their world they can nevertheless experience it as something more than a human construction. This implies that meaning cannot be objective in the positivist sense that meaning is constructed by people. There is an emphasis here on the actor's definition of the situation. It is contended that 'all knowledge and therefore all meaningful reality as such, is contingent upon human practices, being constructed in and out of interaction between human beings and their world, and developed and transmitted within an essentially social context' (Crotty, 1998, p. 42). This means that 'experiences do not constitute a sphere of subjective reality separate from, and in contrast to, the objective realm of the external world – as Descartes' split between mind and body, and thereby mind and world, would lead us to imagine' (ibid., p. 45). It is worth noting that the proposition presented in Chapter 3, that organisational knowledge resides in routines, is based on the belief that knowledge is a social construction, as organisational knowledge comes from organisational members interacting, mutually influencing each other's views, and creating and changing organisationally shared reality constructions (Spender, 1996; Klimecki and Lassleben, 1998).

In summary, the main reason for adopting an interpretive approach in my research was that I needed to find a method that would allow me to take into consideration the idea that the external and internal environments are not objectively knowable – that is, that what counts is the perceived environment and perceived resources and that strategies for and judgements of organisational performance are in the eyes of the beholder. Such a stance meant that I was interested in individual perceptions and not generalisations, and hence needed to find a research method or methods that would allow me to capture the constructed reality of individuals that enabled them to make sense of the world around them. In short I took the position that 'if men define situations as real, they are real in their consequences' (Thomas and Thomas, 1928, p. 572).

## Possible research strategies

As discussed earlier, the theoretical idea that tacit knowledge plays a central part in the development of competitive advantage is widely accepted but there has been little empirical research to support the proposition. One of the main reasons for this is that empirically researching tacit routines is problematic. Research instruments such as surveys and structured interviews are likely to be inappropriate in that individuals cannot be asked to state what they cannot readily articulate and one cannot identify tacit routines by reading documents pertaining to a company's operations (Badaracco, 1991). Therefore my main challenge was to find ways of expressing what to date had been in-expressible (Nonaka, 1991).

As there is no established method of empirically researching tacit routines, before starting my empirical exploration I had to develop a research approach that would enable me to identify such tacit routines and establish whether they were perceived by managers to be a component in their account of their firm's success. The methodology set out below is based on a review of research methods used for intangible phenomena. The material in this chapter is theoretical in that it is the research proposal I designed before embarking on the empirical work. In other words, it is the methodology I developed for eliciting tacit routines. Since people would not be able to report their tacit routines directly it was necessary explore indirect means of representing these routines. Causal mapping promised to be a useful research approach, possibly in combination with Bougon's (1983) self-Q technique and interviews where participants would be encouraged to tell stories and employ metaphors. The suitability of participant observation as a research method was also considered.

Given that tacit routines cannot readily be talked about, the main task was to find a means of identifying them without asking managers about them directly, that is, to find a method that would facilitate the unlocking of tacit routines. Because of the lack of previous research on the issue it was not possible to adopt someone else's method. Therefore I set out the criteria such a method would have to meet and then I searched the literature for a suitable solution. The method would have to enable me to capture tacit routines that could be accessed but not expressed through the normal use of words, as well as tacit routines that had not yet been articulated but could be (see Chapter 4 on the degrees of tacitness), and to establish whether these routines were perceived by managers to be a component of their firm's success. In short I needed a method that would allow for activities/actions to be captured. I also needed a method that would enable me to identify relationships between various routines, and between routines and organisational success. This meant that the method had to be able to cope with representing complicated and detailed activities and the complexity of how organisational members interacted to achieve success. It also had to be powerful enough to trigger managers' memory of how they had done things, and flexible enough to capture routines whenever they surfaced.

These criteria implied the need for a research instrument that would facilitate in-depth capture of organisational routines, and that the use of large sample surveys and secondary data was not a valid option. This led me to consider qualitative methods such as semistructured or unstructured interviews, cognitive mapping (discussed below) and participant observation, as these are known to enable an in-depth understanding of details and the disentangling of what is happening in real settings. The nature of tacit routines, notably their context dependency and uniqueness, also indicated a case study approach, as opposed to a broad sample study, which would not reveal idiosyncratic sources of advantage (Rouse and Daellenbach, 1999). Obviously the case study approach would have drawbacks, notably in terms of result generalisation, but this was of minor concern in view of the interpretive stance adopted, the 'need for a fine-grained analysis inside the firm' (Collis, 1991, p. 50), and the richness of data that could be obtained from a case study.

## Cognitive maps

Cognitive maps are visual ways of representing individuals' views of reality (Eden *et al.*, 1981). They 'are intended to relate to the way in which a person "makes sense of" and explains the world around him' (Eden, 1990, p. 37). They are the representation of an individual's personal knowledge, of her or his own experience (Weick and Bougon, 1986). 'The process of map construction and the use of the map is intended to facilitate the elaboration and exploration by the client of his own belief and value system in relation to particular issues' (Eden *et al.*, 1981, p. 41).

There are various types of cognitive map (see Huff, 1990), one being the cause or causal map: 'a cause map is a form of cognitive map that incorporates concepts tied together by causality relations' (Weick and Bougon, 1986, p. 106). It is a graphic representation that 'consists of nodes and arrows that link them' (Laukannen, 1994, p. 323). The nodes are the constructs that the person believes are important and the arrows show the relationships between the constructs.

### Causal mapping

Causal mapping was likely to be an appropriate technique to use when researching tacit routines because it would enable me to focus on action (Huff, 1990). As discussed earlier, tacit routines are about doing things, they are goal oriented, and in this respect causal mapping would be highly appropriate because 'causality provides a potentially higher level of procedural knowledge (how it works, and how to do it) than other sets of relationships' (Jenkins, 1995, p. 53).

Another reason for using such maps is that the question of whether tacit routines can be a source of success is by nature a causal one. Furthermore causal maps can be particularly useful for eliciting factors that are context-dependent (which tacit routines are) because, 'by virtue of the time spent in a particular department or function, managers develop a viewpoint that is consistent with the activities and goals of that department or particular function' (Walsh, 1988, p. 875), and as Bougon *et al.* (1977) point out, this is partly stored in the minds of managers in the form of causal maps. In short causal maps can reflect what is understood to be happening in an organisation. One of the main advantages of using such a technique is that maps 'place concepts in relation to one another, . . . they impose structure on vague situations' (Weick and Bougon, 1986, p. 107). Causal maps are therefore a way of ordering and analysing something that is 'fuzzy', they establish relationships between factors. They are also useful in eliciting tacit routines because they enable issues to be studied at a micro level, can represent multiple explanations and consequences, and can reveal the interrelationships between factors and potential dilemmas (Eden and Ackermann, 1998).

However causal maps should not be taken as models of cognition as such (Eden *et al.*, 1992). As Eden (1992, p. 262) puts it, 'the only reasonable claim that can be made of cognitive maps as an artefact . . . is that . . . they may represent subjective data more meaningfully than other models'. Hence they should simply be used as a means to reveal tacit routines. This is possible because causal maps are 'content and theory free' and are not 'necessarily linked with the psychological construct of cognitive maps' (Laukannen, 1998, pp. 168, 169).

## Group mapping

According to the literature there are several ways of constructing group or collective maps. They can consist of the average of individual maps, be a composite of individual maps (Weick and Bougon, 1986) or be derived from group discussions (Nelson and Mathews, 1991). Because a group map may encompass more than the combined content of individual maps (Langfield-Smith, 1992), it is suggested here that causal mapping should be a group activity, based on a group discussion. By listening to the views of others and reconsidering their own views, group members should be able to reflect on their own behaviour and that of others in the light of group-level interaction and discussion. Moreover a group map, 'as a visual interactive model, acts in the form of a . . . transitional object, that encourages dialogues' (Eden and Ackermann, 1998, p. 71). This means that the maps are neither a representation of the reality perceived by all in the organisation nor the representation of the reality perceived by one individual, but a collectively constructed account of what is happening.

The idea that 'the process of constructing a consensus around causal factors influencing the organisation can be a useful diagnostic exercise' for the organisation (Nelson and Mathews, 1991, p. 381), added to the fact that a mapping session would only require about half a day of managers' time, could serve to convince organisations to participate in my research. The group discussions could take the form of focus groups. To discover which tacit routines were valuable and to follow the resource-based view of the firm's line of asking 'Is X a resource?', the discussion could focus on the question 'What makes your organisation successful?' Respondents could be asked to describe the relationships between the constructs, decide which variable influenced which other variables and so on. The relationships could be established not only on the basis of what the participants 'knew' and said, but also through their attitudes, reactions, feelings and so on. The advantage of a focus group format was that 'inherent group dynamics tend to yield insights that ordinarily are not obtainable from individual interviews' (Schiffman and Kanuk, 1991, p. 52).

When it came to choosing the group of participants I decided to take the pragmatic line (Easterby-Smith *et al.*, 2000) that only a small number of organisational members would have much influence on the organisational strategy, and therefore working with top and senior managers involved in the operational activities of the firm would provide a reasonable approximation of what was happening in the various parts of the organisation.

# 6

# Revealing Tacit Routines as a Source of Organisational Success: The Process

Causal mapping promised to be powerful way of revealing tacit routines because the process would be about continuously asking the respondents to reflect on their behaviour, on what they did (Ambrosini and Bowman, 2001a,b), something they would not ordinarily do. During the mapping they would be pressed to explain what they did and in the process they should become aware of aspects of their behaviour that previously had been tacit (in terms of degree B and possibly C of tacitness in Figure 4.1, Chapter 4). Thus the in-depth probing that would allow the map to develop should tap the routines that went unspoken in the organisation.

## Starting the causal map

As mentioned in Chapter 5, the process would focus on the question 'What makes your organisation successful?' The first few answers were likely to be well-known causes of success. They were likely to be general and of common knowledge.

There were several alternatives for building up the map. For instance Walsh (1988) used a predefined list, Axelrod (1976) derived the constructs from texts and Markóczy and Goldberg (1995) derived them from interviews. As tacit routines are both context-specific and non-prescribed ways of doing things, predefined checklists or structured interviews were likely to be inappropriate. There was a need to create a situation in which the map would 'emerge as fully as possible with a minimum of influence' (Bougon, 1983, p. 182), that is, it was necessary to 'avoid suggesting anything to the individual that might become part of an eventual cognitive map' (Cossette and Audet, 1992, p. 332). This implied that the map should ideally be built up without predetermined constructs, and that these should be established during the mapping session itself.

However starting a causal mapping session from scratch could be time consuming and preliminary interviews offered a way of eliciting constructs that could be used as a basis for starting the map. The research method literature revealed two techniques that might be appropriate in this respect: self-Q interviews (a technique that minimises the influence of the researcher – see Bougon, 1983), and semistructured interviews with storytelling. Each participant could be interviewed once, with half the group being interviewed using the first technique and half using the second. This dual technique would 'make sure that the ground [was] well covered' (Markóczy and Goldberg, 1995, p. 310). The interviews would be carried out on an individual basis, which should provide the opportunity to establish a rapport with the participants. This would be paramount as 'close rapport with respondents opens doors to more informed research' (Fontana and Frey, 1994, p. 367). The two methods are described in the following sections.

## Self-Q

The self-Q technique is a non-directive approach developed by Bougon (1983). It is a self-interviewing technique that draws on the respondent's account of his or her beliefs in order to generate constructs. The reason why tacit routines might be revealed through self-Q questioning is that 'in self-Q interviews, participants essentially interview themselves. The first key idea is that participants are the experts on the personal knowledge that guides their social behaviour. The second key idea is that participants formulate their questions on the basis of their own personal knowledge . . . and on the basis of their own thinking . . . about the situation they are questioning' (Bougon *et al.*, 1989, pp. 328, 329). '[T]he events, objects, and concepts [the participants] use to express their questions . . . reveal their tacit and explicit knowledge' (ibid., p. 329).

With regard to eliciting constructs that could be used to start building a group map, the technique involves 'people ask[ing] themselves questions about whatever topic is being mapped and the concepts are then extracted from the questions' (Weick and Bougon, 1986, p. 115). Here the questioning focuses on the respondents' thoughts on what they do that makes the organisation successful. Practically, 'the Self-Q technique uses a framing statement and a . . . diagram. The framing statement is read by participants and is intended to set the stage for self-questioning and to provide the subject with enough information to begin the self-questioning process. . . . The diagram is intended to be used by participants to cue themselves to ask additional questions' (Sheetz *et al.*, 1994, p. 37). This technique is appealing because it lowers participants' resistance to making a response: 'people are not practised in defending against questions that they ask themselves and over which they have control. Furthermore, since the person is asking questions rather than making assertions, the questions themselves seem harmless' (Weick and Bougon, 1986, p. 115). Another benefit of the technique is that the researcher does not hinder the production of constructs by his or her lack of knowledge of the organisation being studied. The fact that 'often a researcher . . . does not really know enough to ask the right questions' (Bougon *et al.*, 1989, p. 353) is not an issue when using the self-questioning technique.

## Interviews: storytelling and metaphors

The second method of uncovering constructs is the semistructured interview. Such interviews are semistructured in the sense that their purpose and structure is predetermined. Participants can be encouraged to give examples through storytelling and metaphors.

### Storytelling

It is useful to encourage interviewees to tell stories because 'stories are one of the many forms of implicit communication used in organisational contexts' (Martin, 1982, p. 257). People 'manage the collective memory of the organisation through storytelling' (Boje, 1991a, p. 9). According to Martin (1982, p. 256), stories are used in organisations to 'explain "how things are done around here"'. It is also an appropriate device for studying tacit routines because people frame their experiences in stories (Wilkins and Thompson, 1991). Moreover 'stories are contextually embedded' (Boje, 1991b, p. 109), they 'can reflect the complex social web within which work takes place' (Brown and Dugruid, 1991, p. 44).

Through storytelling employees not only reveal what is done in the organisation, but also tend to say more than they would normally, thus enabling 'researchers to examine perceptions that are often filtered, denied, or not in the subjects' consciousness during traditional interviews' (Hansen and Kahnweiler, 1993, p. 1394). The participants can be asked to tell two stories, one positive and one negative, about what has caused organisational success and organisational failure (this is based on the critical incident technique developed by Flanagan,

1954). As recommended by Ford and Wood (1992), whenever possible the interviews should take place in the participants' organisation as the familiar environment can serve as cues.

## Metaphors

Martin (1982) argues that not only stories but also metaphors can serve to transmit tacit knowledge. Metaphors are an interesting way of revealing tacit routines for a variety of reasons, but before explaining these we shall define the term.

According to Ortony, (1975, p. 45), 'Metaphor involves, or is, the transfer of meaning'. It involves the transfer of information from a relatively familiar domain (usually called the vehicle or the base domain) to a relatively unknown domain, usually called the tenor, the topic or the target domain (Tsoukas, 1991). In other words metaphors allow 'inferences to be made about one of the things, usually that about which we know least, on the basis of what we know about the other' (Harré, 1984, p. 172), that is, the meaning of the vehicle is applied to the topic, the vehicle is used metaphorically, there is a comparison between two terms. The metaphor provides 'information about the structure, content, and meaning of the particular situation' (Sackmann, 1989, p. 465). It is worth noting that a distinction is sometimes made between metaphors (the general term), similes (which compare one item to another – A is like B) and analogies (which focus on the relationship between items – A is to B as C is to D). However in most studies no differentiation is made (Ortony, 1975; Sackmann, 1989).

There are a variety of reasons why it is claimed that metaphors can help to reveal tacit routines. First, metaphorical language can give voice to tacit knowledge (Munby, 1986, p. 198) because 'metaphors can communicate meaning when no explicit language is available, especially in regard to complex ambiguous experience' (Srivastava and Barrett, 1988, p. 60). Second, metaphors can generate new meaning – they can 'render vague and abstract ideas concrete' (Sackmann, 1989, p. 482), and because they allow different ways of thinking they may help people to explain complex organisational phenomena (Tsoukas, 1991). Third, they 'transmit an entire story visually using one image' (Sackmann, 1989, p. 468). This idea of image is central to understanding the articulation of tacit knowledge through metaphors. Because metaphors provide vivid images they can substitute for a large number of words (Sackmann, 1989) and they are 'useful in coping with large amounts of data' (Hill and Levenhagen, 1995, p. 1068). Images also allow us to speak about processes because images can flow from one to another. This matters as tacit routines are *processes* – they are about doing things.

The procedural aspect of tacit activities is one reason why it is difficult to communicate them through words. This is because 'language [is a] discrete symbols system ... words partition experiences' (Ortony, 1975, p. 46). However,

> experience does not arrive in little discrete packets, but flows, leading us imperceptibly from one state to another. . . . Thus the task we have to perform in communication is to convey what is usually some kind of continuum by using discrete symbols. It would not be surprising if discrete symbol systems were incapable of literally capturing every conceivable aspect of an object, event or experience that one might wish to describe ... This deficiency is filled by metaphor (ibid., p. 46).

Metaphors are a means of capturing the continuous flow of experiences, hence they can be a means of capturing tacit ways of doing things. 'They allow the transfer of concrete bands of experience whereas literal discourse segments experiences' (Tsoukas, 1991, p. 581). 'One can say through metaphor what cannot be said in discrete, literal terms, especially when words are not available or do not exist' (Srivastava and Barrett, 1988, p. 37). For instance a designer who attempted to design a cordless food processor described the process of integrating several competing requirements as just like 'watching a film of an exploding shed run in reverse'. Using this metaphor he was able to describe in a few words a complex situation that involved multiple factors.

All this suggests that it is worth considering metaphors when attempting to uncover tacit routines. However the use of metaphors may not be trouble free. One problem is ensuring that a metaphor is used only when more direct language is not possible. One way of doing this is to ask the individual to express his or her metaphor in another way. If another metaphor is used rather than a literal description, then the use of metaphor is appropriate. A second problem is that all individuals may not be willing or able to use metaphors during a discussion.

## Constructing the map

Interviews, whether based on self-Q or conducted on a semistructured basis, should allow the interviewer to get to know the participants, give them confidence in the process and of course elicit a few success factors.

This being done, the process of revealing tacit routines begins in earnest. The map can start with the causes of success identified in the interviews, the goal at this point being to ascertain the reasons for those successes. Appropriate questions to ask the participants are: 'How does that happen?' 'What causes that?' 'Who is involved?' 'What influences that?' The act of answering the questions should enable the participants to start to elicit more precise reasons for the success. This can be likened to peeling an onion: by peeling layer after layer of the reasons for success the participants eventually arrive at the less explicit causes of success, causes they would not have easily identified without prompting and probing.

At this point – when the participants have to reflect on matters they never usually think about – the flow of causal factors is likely to slow down and the participants should be encouraged to think of examples of how they perform the factor they have just elicited, tell stories about the factor or use metaphors to explain how the factor works. As discussed above, this should help them to articulate activities that are difficult to express.

Throughout the mapping the participants should be encouraged to speak about what they do and if possible the factors should be written down as actions rather than abstract statements, as tacit routines are about doing and not verbalising what is done. It is not about 'knowing about' or 'not knowing about'. This will also ensure that the participants will deal with what they currently do, as 'the organisation, within its marketplace, is the way it acts from moment to moment – not the way it thinks it might act or ought to act' (Peters, 1984, p. 11). The mapping is complete when the participants, despite being pressed for more examples and being encouraged to say more, are unable to reveal any more factors.

## The reliability and validity of causal maps

In order to guarantee the quality of the findings it is vital to check their validity and reliability. Furthermore they will have to stand up to outside scrutiny and therefore must be believable. In the following subsections the terms validity and reliability are defined, and it is explained why the findings from causal mapping research can be claimed to be valid and reliable.

### Validity

In positivist studies, where the concept was developed, confirmation of validity is approached by asking 'are we measuring what we think we are measuring?' (Kerlinger, 1973, p. 457), or 'does an instrument measure what it is supposed to measure' (Easterby-Smith *et al.*, 1992, p. 41). However for qualitative and social constructivist research such questions may not be appropriate as 'measurement' implies numbers and an objective reality. As Jenkins (1998, p. 240) points out, 'in the context of causal . . . mapping, this question is clearly difficult to answer . . . Kerlinger's [1973] question can be regarded as a positivistic view of validity. It assumes that there is a reality that can be measured in some way.' Reason and Rowan (1981) suggest that validity can be 'definitional' and does not have to focus solely on measurement. In the context of causal mapping Jenkins (1998, p. 240) proposes that a more appropriate approach to validity is to ask 'have we allowed the respondent to respond in a way which is salient and meaningful to him or her?' This approach gives validity to the method proposed above as the map is constructed by the participants themselves and they are free (and actively encouraged) to introduce whatever ideas they want and to modify the map at any stage.

## Reliability

Reliability is about consistency, replicability and accuracy, so the question is whether there is a 'relative absence of errors of measurement in a measuring instrument' (Kerlinger, 1973, p. 443). In other words, when looking at a study we need to know whether, if it were conducted by somebody else under the same conditions, the results would be the same. Errors can come from various sources, notably the researcher or the participants. In the causal mapping process, possible researcher bias is minimised by the fact that the researcher's involvement is limited. The researcher is merely there to prompt the participants to talk and to record faithfully what they say, with the participants constantly checking what is being recorded. As far as participant bias is concerned, variables such as tiredness, stress and mood can affect the process and therefore producing the same results when replicating the study will involve replicating exactly the same context and conditions, which is extremely difficult.

Mintzberg *et al.* (1976) suggest that tapping the memory of individuals can produce two types of error: distortion and memory failure. With the method proposed above, distortion should not be an issue because causal mapping sessions are group sessions. Any distortion by one individual should be noted by the others in the group and will probably be mentioned as the session is open and people are encouraged to express themselves freely. However there is always the possibility that a participant may deliberately distort the process for his or her own ends, for instance by reporting activities that do not take place, or are not performed in the way articulated. This risk can be kept to a minimum if the session is conducted in a supportive, non-threatening environment. Moreover if there is no compulsion to participate in the session and the participants are there because they want to benefit from it, there will be no point in them deliberately distorting their comments.

Memory failure is certainly more of a possibility, however the way in which the session is conducted should limit this. First, in a group session the participants can be expected to trigger each other's memories. Second, the aim of the session is not to investigate old events but to explore what the participants are currently doing, what they are involved in now and this should be fresh in their memory. Third, the participants are asked to tell stories, present metaphors and give examples. Stories present things sequentially and causally, and hence they should have a snow-ball effect on the participants' memories. Fourth, and this is addressed in the conclusion when dealing with the limitations of the present study, while the aim is to map organisational success it goes without saying that only some of the causes of success can be mapped because (a) there is an obvious time constraint as mapping the entire organisation would take weeks if not months, and (b) the maps are constructed by a limited number of the organisation's managers and therefore only their perceptions of the causes of success are recorded. However if a factor is omitted during the session it should not have a major implication for studies such as that reported in this book because the aim is to map only part of what is happening in the organisation. While this is limiting, it is not a reason for not pursuing the research, considering the present paucity of knowledge on routines. To quote Laukkannen (1998, p. 75) on the validity and reliability of causal mapping, 'the pragmatic conclusion is to do one's best to enhance data quality by acting on areas that are obviously critical and controllable'. By thoroughly researching, thinking about and planning the causal mapping session and its aims, the researcher will have done her or his best in terms of 'measuring' what she or he wants to do.

## Observation

The research proposal established above, using causal mapping and interviews, could be complemented with participant observation as this might enrich the data obtained and improve the validity of the findings (Pettigrew, 1973). As explained in the literature review, tacit routines are picked up by 'osmosis' (Spender, 1996), develop over time (Leonard-Barton, 1992), are acquired through experience (Ravetz, 1971) and are acquired where used (Wright, 1994). For these reasons Pavitt (1991) has suggested that the most effective way of learning tacit routines is through personal contact and discussions. Pursuing the same line, Sobol and Lei (1994, p. 171) declare that 'learning tacit knowledge and routines requires continuous day-to-day contact with the person, team or organisation possessing such knowledge through an apprentice-like relationship where the routines are directly observed and practiced'.

All this suggests that research into tacit routines could be conducted through observation of and immersion in an organisation, notably because 'observation is justified if no language or vocabulary is available with which to describe that native experience in which the ethnographer is interested' (Werner and Schoepfle, 1987, p. 266). Participant observation takes the researcher inside the organisation, allowing her or him to gain in-depth knowledge about organisational processes as well as an understanding of the context. However as the context is changed by the inquiry process, observation as a method implies the need to spend quite some time in the organisation so that the disruptive effect dissipates. Another option is to follow Louis and Bartunek's (1992) suggestion of having research teams composed of both insiders and outsiders. They believe that such teams are useful when the research goal is 'to explicate core beliefs and/or assumptions held by a member of a setting' (ibid., p. 108).

Observation and causal mapping can therefore complement each other and provide a rich picture of the organisation being studied. However even if time is not an issue, direct observation of skilful performances is likely to be complicated when researching tacit routines. It would be impossible to be everywhere at once (a large team would be required to watch many individuals in the organisation) and the observer may not necessarily understand the significance of the activities being carried out. Furthermore the observation may be so limited that it would be difficult to relate what was being observed to organisational-level success. The causal mapping method described earlier is an indirect way of surfacing tacit routines. The map may be fragmented, incomprehensive, partial and biased, but it can provide some insights into tacit routines and organisational success.

## Conclusion

This chapter has proposed an approach for empirical research into tacit routines. This approach is based on a general review of the research

1.  Conduct preliminary self-Q and semistructured interviews based on storytelling and metaphors about the causes of success in the organisation in order to elicit constructs to start the causal map (A, B and C).

2.  Start the map with the success factors revealed during the interviews.

3.  Elicit tacit routines with questions such as 'What causes that?' 'How does it happen?'

4.  If the flow of constructs stops, ask questions such as 'Could you give an example of how that happened?' 'Could you tell a story?'

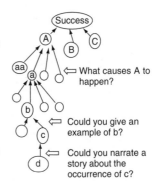

*Figure 6.1*   Researching tacit routines as a component of firms' success: summary of the proposed method (adapted from Ambrosini and Bowman, 2001a)

methodology literature as tacit routines have not been explored previously and hence no empirically tested method can be adopted. It has been suggested that causal mapping could be a useful method to assess whether tacit routines are a source of sustainable competitive advantage. The causal mapping process, facilitated by encouraging the participants to tell stories and employ metaphors, should enable the participants to uncover and describe routines they would not normally talk about. Figure 6.1 summarises the methodology.

The next chapter explains how this methodology was applied and what was learnt from using it in the field.

# Part IV

# The Research Project: Investigating Tacit Routines

# 7

# Stage 1: Identifying Organisational Tacit Knowledge as a Component of Firms' Success

This chapter and Chapters 8–12 are dedicated to the empirical work carried out using the approach and definitions established in the previous chapters.

## The first study: Alpha

### Background

The first organisation studied was is a UK-based mutual organisation, which in this book is given the pseudonym Alpha. Alpha is the UK's leading provider of occupational pension schemes for charities, voluntary bodies and not-for-profit organisations. It is managed by a chief executive and his team, and is overseen by a board of trustees. Alpha was selected for two main reasons: it was keen to take part in the study, and it was successful. The CEO of the organisation explained that his organisation had performed very well over the past five years in terms of membership growth, investment performance and customer satisfaction, that it was the fastest-growing pension provider in the UK and that within the industry, and its niche market in particular, it had a strong reputation and was well regarded.

The full top management team participated in the study. The team was composed of the chief executive, the deputy chief executive, the human resources director, the business development director and the finance director, all of whom were interested in the project because they wanted fully to understand the causes of their success. This was particularly so because they were embarking on a change programme involving the use of new technologies to improve efficiency, a cost-cutting exercise, a new set of products for their customers and the opening of a new site. This set of changes was coupled with a growth plan – they aimed to double their membership. Before progressing further with the implementation of their plans the management team thought it would be valuable to learn as much as possible about their current bases of success in order to protect them and possibly build on them in the future. Another impetus was to be able better to explain Alpha's position to the board of trustees that governed the organisation.

## Eliciting tacit activities at Alpha

### The interviews

As outlined in the methodology chapters, in order to start the process of uncovering the routines that mattered for Alpha's success I first conducted interviews with each of the team members and asked what they believed to be the reasons for their organisation's success. In line with the theoretical protocol, two were interviewed using Bougon's self-Q technique and semistructured interviews were used for the other three. The protocols for both types of interview can be found in Appendix 1. During the interviews I took notes of the factors mentioned and comments made. I then drew up a list of the factors that were thought to contribute to the organisation's success. This list contained 63 elements (see Appendix 2) that could be grouped into themes or generic factors. The list was too long to explore fully as the causal mapping session was planned to last just one day. Consequently I decided to ask the team to map the most frequently cited factors. They were:

- Big clients joining.
- CEO.
- Charity market.
- Customer focus.
- Ethos.
- Investment returns.
- Services offered.
- Staff commitment.
- Trustees.

### The causal mapping session

Just under three weeks later the top management team was invited to take part in a causal mapping session to reveal the routines that were making Alpha successful. The research team consisted of myself and two other facilitators, who would share the task of questioning, recording and reflecting on what was being said. One person would be in charge of the recording and the other two would do most of the facilitating. Notes would also be taken on the general running of the event.

At the start of the workshop the participants were handed the nine-item list of causes of success elicited during the interviews. They were then reminded of how the day was to proceed and that the aim of the session was to uncover the reasons for Alpha's success, and in particular the routines that caused the nine factors to lead to success.

It was emphasised that we were only interested in things that they were currently doing – even if these were perceived to be trivial or irrelevant – and not in what they believed they should be doing. It was important to stress that anything could (and should) be said, even if it was perceived as insignificant, as it was likely that the factors that were leading to relative success (considering the resource-based view of the firm's argument) did not reside in obvious generic factors but in the detail, in the idiosyncratic ways of doing things in the organisation. They were also asked to concentrate on what they thought was unique to their organisation. Finally, they were told that they had to make links between the various activities mentioned.

In order to keep the mapping process going we kept asking the participants questions, especially when they were struggling to think of reasons for success. The questions included 'How does that happen?' 'What causes that?' 'Who is involved?' 'What influences that?' 'Could you please give us an example?' All the questions were kept simple and to the point.

To help with the mapping process we employed Decision Explorer software (a Windows-based mapping software developed by Colin Eden, Fran Ackermann and their colleagues at the University of Strathclyde). The map was displayed on a screen so that the participants could see it evolving. Too much data was collected to fit on one map and therefore we concentrated on a proportion of the factors at a time and generated a number of maps. At the end of the session the maps were printed and each individual received copies (see Appendix 3).

Whether a routine was tacit or not could only be assessed by the individuals concerned as a routine may have been tacit for some managers but not for others. For instance, if during the group session it was revealed that the activity 'Speaking to customers without recording the message' was a source of success, one needed to know whether all the managers had been aware of that before the session. This suggested that the maps should be coded. Hence at the end of the mapping session each participant was requested to individually code the maps according to the following categories:

- Routines that are well known to you.
- Routines that are known about but that you find difficult to deal with.
- Routines that were tacit to you until the group session.

The participants were also provided with definitions of these categories, as shown in Table 7.1.

In the methodology decided upon before the session there were two categories rather than three. The third one, B, emerged in the course of

*Table 7.1*   Working definitions of the coding categories

| Coding categories | Working definitions |
| --- | --- |
| A. Routines that are well known to you | Please mark with the letter A all those activities which you are aware are going on in the organisation and which you understand. |
| B. Routines that are known about but that you find difficult to deal with | Please mark with the letter B all those activities which you know are going on in the organisation and matter, but which tend to be left as they are. This could be because no one really knows how to manage or change them. For instance you know that it is important for the organisation to have good relationships between salespersons and clients, however nobody in the organisation really knows how to improve these relationships. |
| C. Routines that were tacit to you until the group session | Please mark with the letter C all those things which you are doing but did not realise you were doing. An activity is tacit if until now you were involved in this activity but never described or discussed it. For instance you did not realise that you always shake hands with female and male clients alike and that this is appreciated by the female clients and has helped to build up good client–supplier relationships. |

the session. During one of the breaks I was talking with the participants about their experiences when one of them mentioned her surprise about how little the top management team actually managed the routines that had been elicited. When asked what she meant she explained that she was aware of many of these routines, and knew they were important to Alpha's success, but that she had left them to take their own course because she did not really know how they worked. This is what prompted me to include the additional category.

## The results

### Results from the coding

The team generated such a large amount of data during the session that it was decided they should concentrate on just four maps (see Appendix 3, Figures A3. 4–7). Two of the participants failed to return their maps, despite being prompted. However the chief executive, the human resources director and the business development director did return their sets, which meant that I had 12 maps to work on.

During the mapping session I had not always stopped the participants talking about things that were wrong at Alpha, so in order to respect my research question I had to make sure that all routines that were not positive were removed before carrying out the analysis. These included routines that were perceived as a hindrance to the organisation's success and things the team members wished they did rather than what they actually did. For instance, statements such as 'We are losing experienced people' and 'Replace N2 qualified employees with N4 grades' were excluded from the analysis.

As this study was exploratory and I had been able to find no evidence of previous empirical research on the part played by tacit routines in competitive advantage, I had very few working hypotheses. Based on the literature, and on the problems linked to eliciting tacit routines, I had thought that the large majority of factors would be coded A (explicit routines), and that only one or two would be allotted to category C (tacit routines). In the event the coding varied from one participant to another, so aggregating the individual data would be meaningless. The CEO and business development director put the largest of proportion factors into category A (53.7 per cent and 54.4 per cent respectively). The CEO coded all the factors as A or B, while the business development director put 89.5 per cent of the factors into these two categories. Examples of factors coded as B (known about but difficult to deal with)

included 'Young staff profile' (CEO) and 'They trust us (poor performance is a blip)' (business development director).

The human resources director's codings were significantly different.
Indeed he allotted only 28.6 per cent of the factors to category A and
a total of just 37.3 per cent to A, B or both. In other words, for him a
large proportion of the factors were tacit (40.5 per cent versus 0 per
cent and 10.5 per cent for the others). Two factors that he codified as
tacit were 'We understand it, competitors do not', and 'Management
practices which embody the best of both commercial and voluntary
sector'.

The divergent responses were to a certain extent surprising as the top
management team was small and had been together for at least three
years. This suggests that what is tacit may only be tacit for one or two
directors of an organisation. This is confirmed by looking at how each
factor was coded. Indeed no factors were seen as tacit by all three team
members and only three factors (out of 20) were recognised as tacit by
two of them. One of these factors was 'The bigger the client, the more
people want to get involved'. Moreover only three factors were deemed
to belong to B by the CEO and the two directors, including 'Different
modes of behaviour are acceptable in different areas', and six were allotted
to B by two of the team members, including 'We can go on gut-feeling,
we don't take a commercial view'. This indicates that perceptions of tacitness are personal and not organisational, but each team member had a
different functional background and occupation, it could be functionally biased (Walsh, 1988).

The analysis of the coding also revealed that a fair proportion of the
success factors at Alpha were perceived as difficult to deal with (category
B). The chief executive put 46 per cent of the factors in this category,
the business development director 35 per cent and the human resources
director 31 per cent. Statements that were allotted to category B
included:

- 'Get it right first time.'
- 'We write customers a 10-page letter instead of two pages.'
- 'The way in which managers and team leaders behave.'

### Lessons learnt from the results

The following subsections consider the lessons learnt from the results
and the coding procedure, and what Alpha's top management team
discovered about the causes of success in their organisation.

*Lessons learnt from the results and coding*

One conclusion to be drawn from my experience with Alpha is that the participants need to code the maps on their own. I need to keep the coding individual. From one manager to another there was a large difference between the number of factors coded and between the factors coded as tacit. There is also the question of whether the factors coded as tacit were actually tacit. Was it possible that the participants were unaware of the existence of some of the factors? Tacit factors are actions that are not verbalised. They are activities that people in the organisation carry out but have never talked about. This suggests that another category is required: 'Routines you did not know about', that is, a category that deals with ignorance. Returning to the initial definition: tacit routines are about doing and not verbalising what is done, it is not about 'knowing about' or 'not knowing about'.

At this point I would like to make another comment on the definition of tacit routines. As discussed earlier, in the strategy literature it is usually presumed that there is no separation between tacit knowledge and valuable performance, that they form a whole, and therefore tacit knowledge assumes performance. This failure to separate cause and effect is unhelpful for two reasons. First, it could suggest that tacit routines are always valuable, but it has been well argued that they are not always so (Leonard-Barton, 1992) – tacit knowledge can lead to poor performance as well as good performance. Second, it does not allow us to provide a precise enough definition of routines and their relation to performance, it does not allow us to be clear about what is tacit, explicit or ignored. Prompted by the results from the Alpha case I considered possible variations in the relation between tacit routines and performance. Figure 7.1 includes a list of situations that might be faced. It is an elaboration of the concept of tacit routines as source of sustainable competitive advantage, and it should provide more clarity about the nature of tacit routines and assist with further empirical and theoretical development.

Figure 7.1 depicts a very simple situation as only three individuals are involved and the routine only takes place between two persons, while most organisational activities involve more people and most organisations have more than three members. However it demonstrates that one needs to be clear about what is meant by tacit routines, and notably what is tacit to whom. It shows that a routine can only be tacit to those involved in the routine – the 'doers' – and that it may not be tacit to all those involved. As a corollary it also shows that a routine may be either known or ignored by organisational members who are not involved in the routine.

Consider three organisational members – A, B and C – and one routine between A and B. C is not involved in the activity and it is assumed that the routine between A and B has a positive effect on organisational performance.

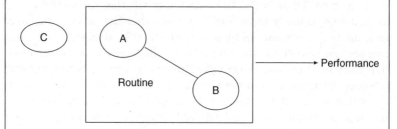

1. Let us first consider the routine on its own. The routine between A and B may be:
- Tacit to both A and B and explicit to C.
- Tacit to both A and B and not known by C.
- Tacit to A, explicit to B and explicit to C.
- Tacit to B, explicit to A and explicit to C.
- Tacit to A, explicit to B and not known by C.
- Tacit to B, explicit to A and not known by C.

2. Let us now consider the routine and its relation to success. The link between the routine and performance may be:
- Tacit to both A and B and explicit to C.
- Tacit to both A and B and not known by C.
- Not known by A, tacit to B and explicit to C.
- Not known by A, tacit to B and not known by C.
- Tacit to A, not known by B and not known by C.
- Tacit to A, not known by B and explicit to C.
- Not known by A, not known by B and explicit to C.
- Not known by A, not known by B and not known by C.

*Figure 7.1*   An elaboration of the concept of tacit routines

As far as the link with performance is concerned, Figure 7.1 illustrates that for any activity the doers may know that the routine they are involved in is linked to performance, may ignore this link, or it may be tacit to them. Once again all the doers may not be in the same situation, for example the link may be known by one but not by another. For those organisational members who are not involved in the activity the situation is simple: they either know about the link or they do not.

Returning to the subject of coding, at the start of the Alpha analysis I encountered a problem I had not anticipated and which needed to be addressed: some factors were left uncoded. There are various possible reasons for this:

- The coding categories proposed may not have been adequate (this might mean asking future participants to state why they have chosen not to code a particular factor, or providing an open category such as 'Other – please specify').
- Some of the participants may have been reluctant to code the factors because they did not care to admit that they did not understand everything that was happening in the organisation. This appears to have been the case with one of the Alpha team members who refused to return the maps and claimed he had learnt nothing from the session, despite displaying great enthusiasm at the end of the day about the value of the exercise. This indicates a need to stress that the exercise is a challenge but there is no right or wrong and the participants need not be afraid of losing face. This also reinforces the view that a high degree of trust is required among the team members and between the team and the researcher.
- The lack of coding, as indicated in discussions with the team afterwards, could also have been due to the fact that it was time consuming.
- The participants may have seen little value in the coding. Creating categories is very much an academic interest and is of little concern to managers. They do not need to know about the nature of the constructs they have revealed. What matters to them is what generates success in their organisation, why it is so and how it can be sustained and developed, and not who knew what and what type of routine it was.

### What the Alpha team learnt

My own concern was not to look at the precise content of the session in terms of helping the Alpha management team with their strategy, rather it was to discover more about tacit activities and whether they were a source of competitive advantage. Nonetheless the team found the experience useful in precise and practical terms for Alpha's strategic direction. As stated earlier, many of the factors that were mapped were straightforward and well known, but some very interesting new issues emerged.

One of these was the recognition by the management team and the CEO himself that his role was central, not in terms of his position but in terms of who he was. The organisation was very dependent on his personality, his contacts, his reputation and his vision of the future. This was so strong that his name was actually perceived as being synonymous with the organisation. Recognising that he played such a vital part in the organisation was particularly important, especially as he was nearing the end of his career. It became clear that succession issues would have to be dealt with very carefully as a poor choice could adversely affect the future of the organisation.

In addition factors such as 'Bachelor status, they can burn the hours' and 'We have a young staff profile' revealed a young, single-person subculture, which combined with the explicit commitment and achievement targets set by the organisation led to employees going voluntarily to work (without extra pay) at weekends or staying late in the evening to beat their targets or to clear backlogs. This helped the team in a later debate about relocating outside London. The young employees did not mind going to work at weekends because Alpha was situated in central London and therefore was close to shops and the London night life. For these young people, working was part of their social life, recognition of which helped the management team to understand why things that had seemed trivial – such as not providing free biscuits – had created real discontent in the organisation. This action went against the subculture, and the management team had not realised that this subculture was so important to the organisation. Not respecting it could lead to loss of commitment and thence to poorer organisational performance.

Finally, factors such as 'Balance between the commercial and voluntary sectors' and 'Management practices that embody the best of both' highlighted the delicate situation Alpha was facing. It was a mutual, not-for-profit organisation that had been established to serve the charity sector. Its mutual status required it to deliver the best service for its members, that is, to provide them with the best possible returns on their investment at the lowest possible cost. This meant that Alpha had a dual responsibility. It had to be professional in its handling of investments, staff control and so on, but at the same time it had to show the charities it had a 'human face' and that it understood and shared their values.

Discussing these conflicting pressures revealed previously tacit aspects of staff recruitment and management styles. For example the person who recruited sales persons apparently asked applicants about their political views. If they were sympathetic to the Labour Party she judged that their values were likely to be aligned with those held by their charity clients. Prior to the mapping session this valuable routine had not been known by others and those recruited had never reflected on her action.

## Conclusions

### Identification of the role of tacit routines in firms' success

The first conclusion is that exploring tacit routines is possible. The causal mapping session conducted at Alpha revealed routines that were tacit to the Alpha's top management team, in other words they perceived that tacit routines played a part in their organisation's success. Causal mapping, in the light of this initial study, appears to be a useful method of revealing tacit routines. The technique allowed the participants to reflect on what they were doing, and by continually being asked what it was they did that caused success the management team brought to light routines they would not normally talk about.

I am obviously aware of the limitations of this case and do not claim that one can establish a unique and direct link between tacit routines and competitive advantage (for more details see the limitations discussed in the concluding chapter). Rather I wish to show that some tacit routines are perceived by managers to be a component of their firm's success.

The case study has shown that there are avenues for empirically researching tacit routines. This means that we can address Rao's (1994) and Jensen's (1993) remarks that 'despite widespread agreement among organisational researchers that intangible resources underlie performance differences among organisations, little empirical evidence exists in the literature' (Rao, 1994, p. 29), and there is a 'need to know much more empirically about the nature of tacit knowledge for it to become a theoretically coherent and convincing . . . construct' (Jensen, 1993, p. 90).

### Unmanaged routines

Perhaps the most surprising finding for the Alpha management team and me was the number of routines that were known about but not effectively dealt with. Despite being important these routines were left alone, they were essentially unmanaged. For the management team this was the major lesson learnt from the exercise as they had never realised that part of why their organisation was successful lay outside their direct management and control. This finding shows that researching routines is valuable and that the benefit for managers is not finding out what is tacit and what is not (this is of more interest to academics) but gaining a better understanding of how their organisation works and knowing what they 'manage' or need to manage in order to help the organisation sustain its advantage.

## Summary

This first case study was very useful. It showed that tacit routines can be a component of firms' success and that causal mapping is a useful technique for empirically researching such routines. The case study also helped me to refine the definition of organisational tacit knowledge and tacit routines by showing that it is important to ask, tacit to whom? One activity may be tacit to some of those who perform it but not to others.

Another finding was that tacit routines are not the only types of activity that play a crucial role, but before considering this issue we shall look at how the method for exploring routines was refined, based on the lessons learnt from the first case study.

# 8
# Stage 2: Methodological Development – Refining the Research Process

The Alpha study indicated that it would be beneficial to learn more about how to conduct causal mapping sessions and that further experience would enable me to gain a better understanding of the process described in Chapter 6. I therefore undertook several mapping exercises, the aim of which was to develop the causal mapping process rather than to learn more about tacit routines as such. Before describing these exercises I shall outline what I learnt from the Alpha case with respect to methodology.

## Methodological lessons

### Lessons learnt from the preliminary interviews

First, self-Q is difficult to use. It is not a natural process and even when the participants at Alpha understood the idea they had a problem with asking questions spontaneously. A flow was never reached and very few factors were generated in comparison with what emerged in the semi-structured interviews. The technique was also time-consuming as the participants had to be briefed in depth. Consequently I abandoned self-Q in the subsequent studies.

Second, the interviews proved a useful ice-breaker. They allowed the participants to get to know the facilitator and the facilitator to learn about the business in which the participants were operating. They also allowed the facilitator to introduce the concepts of tacit knowledge, tacit routines and causal mapping. While the interviews were perhaps not essential, doing without them would have meant spending more time with the group as a whole before the mapping session in order to discuss the exercise and talk about the obvious causes of the business's success. However in cases where access is restricted, the latter method would be as good an option as interviewing the participants beforehand.

Finally, constructing a causal map with the group of managers at Alpha was a fruitful exercise as the managers challenged each other, and something said by one triggered others to produce useful insights.

## Lessons learnt from the causal mapping process

First, it seems that trust and confidence among the participants is essential during the mapping process. They must be relaxed and feel confident and comfortable about expressing themselves, and certain that they will not be made to feel foolish. Otherwise they may not be able to air their intuitive understandings or feelings, and they may just talk about more obvious aspects of their organisation. This would render the exercise a waste of time.

Second, as discussed earlier, metaphors seem to be a powerful tool to expose tacit knowledge, but in practice identifying them is troublesome. In the flow of discussion during the mapping session they are difficult to spot, and even when spotted they are difficult to analyse. One needs to take note of them and come back to them for explanation. However this can sometimes be done immediately so it is worth trying to capture them as they can be a powerful means of expression.

Third, it is crucial during the mapping session to note instances of individuals expressing themselves as follows: 'Oh yes, that's right.' 'Ah! I hadn't realised that.' The 'Oh, yes' acknowledgement indicates that something that was tacit has just been made explicit. It is also a sign that the session is going well and that the participants are gaining insights and becoming aware of their previously tacit routines.

Fourth, the study at Alpha made me realise that while the causal mapping session needs to be kept informal in order not to disturb the flow of ideas, one needs to be directive in that it is important for the participants to be made to deal with what they *currently* do, even if it is perceived to be trivial or irrelevant, and not with what they believe they *should* be doing, which is an understandable concern of organisational members. Asking participants to use verbs is a way of making sure that they are discussing routines, activities in which they are involved. It compels the participants to focus on 'doing'.

Fifth, it is vital to ensure that if success is what is being explored, the participants remain focused on present successes. At Alpha there was a tendency for some of the participants to state what they thought should be done in the organisation, rather than describe actual activities, and to delve into what was not working and what should be done to remedy it.

Sixth, it is worth stressing that asking participants to think of particular examples and tell stories can trigger a lot of constructs. Being required to tell stories forces the participants to explain what is really happening and to provide details. It also triggers other thoughts and stories and hence keeps 'the ball rolling'.

Seventh, as I was not efficient at operating the Decision Explorer software on the spot it slowed the session at Alpha and distracted everybody. We were also too dependent on the technology working perfectly and any hitches were disruptive. As an alternative, self-adhesive notes and large sheets of paper are easy to use, can be easily moved about and should be reliable whatever the situation. Decision Explorer could be used to generate the maps after the session even if the operator is not overly conversant with the software, as it is easy to use.

Finally, the participants, my two colleagues and I found the mapping process very tiring. It went on for almost eight hours and the participants were quite exhausted at the end. They had not expected this and had thought that the exercise would be quite straightforward.

The following sections explain how I added to my experience of conducting causal mapping and how this enabled me to refine my research method.

## Beta

The first opportunity to explore my research method further was provided by 'Beta', a regional newspaper publisher whose managers wanted to identify all the factors that were contributing to their sales performance. A colleague conducted the mapping session while I assisted him and observed what was happening. The whole senior management team of 13 took part in the session. The participants were first asked to list all the well-understood factors that were contributing to Beta's current sales performance. This exercise was useful in eliciting the most obvious causes of success, such as editorial content, the advertising and job sections, the newsagent network, the home delivery, the knowledge of the staff, the achievement of deadlines and so on. Then in small groups the participants were asked to draw a causal map of a few of these factors in order to probe them in depth. It was necessary to divide the group into smaller units because we felt that a 13-member group was too large to allow a smooth-running mapping session.

This study was beneficial in terms of realising that causal mapping is an adaptable technique whose process is easy to explain and which facilitates the identification of what is taken for granted in organisations. It also showed the participants that the causes of success are complex and that they only partially understood the ins and outs of their organisation's success. The session revealed how the different parts of Beta worked collaboratively and effectively to produce enhanced performance. This was part of their ethos. The success factors uncovered included the following: 'There is a lot of goodwill, people are prepared to go out of their way', 'Journalists will choose local rather than national news without thinking about it', 'The departments work well together', 'We understand each other's department's needs', 'We all respect each other, junior to top'.

Another important lesson learnt from the Beta study was that facilitators are essential for such exercises. At Beta the mapping was undertaken by several groups, one of which had a facilitator while the others were left on their own or were merely observed. In the absence of help, of somebody to ask questions and request examples, the participants tended to reach a dead end quickly and were not able to progress further. They also had difficulty carrying out the task and the maps constructed without facilitation were much less detailed than those constructed with assistance. The unfacilitated groups' difficulties were certainly due to the fact that the task was complicated, and that in order to uncover their ways of doing things the managers had to verbalise what they may have never verbalised before and may have been unfamiliar or unknown to others. This is difficult enough to do with a facilitator, but it is even more difficult without one. Without a facilitator to ask questions and request explanations or examples it is difficult for managers to express what they largely take for granted. The facilitator acts as a catalyst, a stimulus that triggers the memory.

Another mapping problem faced with Beta's unfacilitated groups was the use of abbreviations and jargon. Without an outsider to ask for explanations during the mapping session, the maps produced were difficult to understand by anybody from outside the company.

Finally, as at Alpha, fatigue proved a problem. It seems that giving up is likely to occur earlier with unfacilitated groups. If one member becomes tired or frustrated, without a facilitator to maintain the momentum and bring some enthusiasm to the process the rest of the participants are likely to want to stop working.

## Gamma

'Gamma' encompassed two cases and I attended two workshops on two days. The businesses involved were both subsidiaries of a large international industrial group that was engaged in corporate strategic change and wanted to identify the characteristics of its most successful subsidiaries. The aim of the exercise was to reveal the core competences of the subsidiaries using causal mapping. I was there as an observer rather than a facilitator, but the technique used was very similar to the one I had developed. The workshop started with the participants comparing their organisation with its competitors in respect of the factors that mattered most to their customers. Afterwards the participants, with the help of a facilitator, mapped the factors that were thought to enable their organisation to perform better than its competitors.

Attending these workshops was useful for several reasons. For a start the facilitators used my approach. They asked the participants 'What causes that?', and they encouraged them to tell stories and give examples. As I had previously found, the use of examples was a very powerful way of generating understanding of what was happening in the organisation. I also discovered that it was important to pay attention to group composition. In one instance it was very clear that rather than there being a group discussion, one participant was dominating the proceedings. He gave his views and the others acquiesced. They were also quick to back off if this person disagreed with them. This situation was detrimental to the mapping process as the completed map was rather superficial and did not reveal as much as it could have done. The discussion remained rather formal and the participants did not challenge each other.

The workshops also confirmed that it is important to keep participants 'fresh'. The causal mapping process was tiring and as soon as the participants grew tired they stopped delving. Instead they presented obvious factors, made non-challenging comments and wanted to speak about what they knew best. With time and tiredness the participants also tended to speak more about what was wrong with their organisation – focusing on the positive became difficult for them after a few hours of mapping.

## Paul

In Chapter 7, when drawing lessons from my experience at Alpha, I commented that during the process of eliciting tacit routines the managers tended to jog each other's memory. This led me to conclude that a causal mapping session should be conducted with a group rather than individuals as the final map would not have been as rich if individual maps had been aggregated. In order to confirm this I attempted to construct a causal map with the head of a management development business ('Paul').

I asked Paul questions such as 'Why do think that your organisation is successful?' 'Why does it win business?' 'What reasons are unique to your centre?' 'What causes them to happen?' 'What activities do you undertake that make them happen?' 'Could you give me examples of how it works?' The completed map revealed no tacit routines as the data obtained had been explicit and consisted only of what Paul wanted me to know. There are several possible explanations of this, some of which can be linked to Paul himself. He might have wanted to show how good a manager he was. He might have wanted to show that he was in control and was therefore not going to reveal anything that would jeopardise his status. If Paul wanted to distort what was happening in his centre he could do so because he was on his own, and therefore it can be thought that the reliability of a single individual map could be questioned.

Paul may have been unable to bring forth his tacit ways of doing things simply because he was on his own. Human memory does not work linearly but uses association for memory search (Laukannen, 1998). While my questions did trigger Paul's memory, a group of participants who were aware of the context would have acted as a more powerful trigger and their combined effort would have produced a larger range of factors, with one individual triggering a chain of factors from the others. This happened often at Alpha. The other advantage of a group session is that facilitator interference is less as a group dynamic replaces the facilitator's constant questioning. In short, this experience with Paul confirmed that causal mapping should be conducted with a group.

## Insights into causal mapping

In addition to the cases just described, I developed my grasp of the causal mapping process with a group of Masters of Business Administration alumni and a group of managers attending a short course. In both situations the participants engaged in a limited mapping exercise for their own firm and shared their insights and experiences in small groups.

After the workshops with Beta, Gamma and these two groups, I asked the participants what they thought of the process and what they had learnt from it. The findings of the consequent discussions are reported in the two lists below. The first sets out the insights the participants gained from the process and the second addresses the difficulties they encountered.

*Benefits*

- The causal mapping process fosters understanding – it facilitates insights into what is happening in the organisation.
- It places value in the detail and forces participants to deal with specifics.
- It highlights how difficult it is to know what causes success.
- It reveals the 'hot buttons', the key contributors to success.
- It aids understanding of the uniqueness of the organisation – the success factors identified are mostly context-specific.
- It reveals the hidden strengths of the organisation.
- It clarifies interrelationships. Because the map is visual, complex interrelationships can be seen more clearly.
- It highlights the fact that the causes of success in an organisation are not attributable to one division, function or person. All elements are interlocked, and the way in which success is generated cannot be understood by looking at one element in isolation (this is in line with the argument that core competences are not discrete functions or technologies – see Prahalad and Hamel, 1990).
- It shows the importance of people, that people form the basis of success, not equipment and so on (this is in line with the argument that what matters most in an organisation is its people – see Pfeffer, 1995; Pfeffer and Veiga, 1999).
- It focuses on the positive, which is not often done in organisations.
- It identifies crucial processes that are unmanaged, unplanned, unrecognised as mattering and sometimes not well respected in the organisation.
- It shows what the organisation needs to keep doing.
- It provides new ways of discussing strategy and the business process.

*Difficulties*

- The map is very complex – there are a lot of interrelationships so it is difficult to focus and to determine which connections really matter.
- There is a danger of getting bogged down in the detail.
- It may become so complicated that the wood cannot be seen for the trees. Where should the map end?
- It is to some extent reductionist. It is all about those involved in the process, hence it may be biased or too subjective, so perhaps more people need to be involved in the process.
- Who controls the mapping process? Is there a dominant personality? Is the map a representation of the view of one specific group or

individual? In this respect the composition of the group could be important as people may behave differently depending on who is in the group. If the boss is around and dominant, then there is little debate. Moreover 'the degree to which the actor is informed about the events, history, education and local culture determine what actors can or are willing to reveal to us' (Kamann, 1998, p. 81).

- The participants may have a preconceived idea of where the map is going to go.
- Participants have to be honest if the session is to be valuable.
- It is difficult to open up – it can be personally uncomfortable because it makes people realise that they do not know something and admitting this would show that they are not in control.
- The process is time-consuming and it is difficult for managers to get to the specifics of what is happening in their organisation.
- How is the process taken forward? What do the participants do with the maps? How do they report back to the organisation?

## A proposal for facilitating the process

As pointed out by Ackerman (1996), each workshop is unique and therefore it is impossible to predict how the process will work, or how much direction, encouragement and questioning will be needed before the actual session. It is necessary to be able to adapt, especially if the group stagnates quickly or cannot get into the process of mapping their routines. There are numerous publications on facilitating group work (for example Westley and Waters, 1988; Ackerman, 1996), and based on these and my own experiences I suggest that the process should proceed as follows.

As suggested by Eden and Ackerman (1998) the session should start with the facilitator explaining what is going to happen. It is necessary to make sure that the participants are clear about the concept of tacit routines, the goal of the exercise, the mapping process and the coding. Hence the facilitator should (informally) outline the basic principles of tacit routines and the part they play in a firm's success. It is also necessary for the participants to understand the facilitator's role – the facilitator is there to ask questions and write down what they say but not to provide answers or judge anything.

The mapping process should clearly be explained to the participants. They should understand that at the start of the mapping they will be concentrating on what they perceive as the main reasons for their organisation's success. Then the focus will be on unpacking these factors, finding the causes of the reasons for success. To ensure this is well understood the facilitator should provide an example, and present the idea of peeling an onion layer after layer until the conclusion is reached. It should also be explained that the mapping is based on the simple process of the facilitator writing verbatim the suggested factors on self-adhesive stickers, placing these on a large sheet of paper pinned to the wall, and drawing links between the factors, these links being proposed by the participants. The facilitator must also assert that the participants can contribute freely as no record of who said what is taken, that all factors have the same weight, no matter who presents them, and that there is no question of anything being judged right or wrong.

As causal mapping is a tiring process it is important to maintain the level of interest and enthusiasm. Asking questions, and probing for examples can help. Another method is to change the success factor being studied. If the group cannot stay focused on one factor it is worth leaving it, dealing with another and then coming back to it later. The facilitator must remain energetic throughout as any sign of tiredness or lack of commitment will be quickly perceived and spread to the group. For the same reason it is essential to be alert to any verbal or non-verbal sign that somebody is 'switching off', and then to ensure that they are brought back into the discussion. Calling a short break is a simple remedy if changing factors has no effect.

When the allotted time is up or the team is too tired to go on, or when the identified success factors have been examined as fully as possible, then the session can finish. Before the participants are thanked for their efforts they should be reminded that their maps will be properly drawn up, printed and sent to each of them for coding and any additional comments they wish to make.

## Conclusion

In concluding this chapter I would like to point out that the method presented above accords with the interpretive stance adopted for my research (see Chapter 5). As we saw in Chapter 4, I opted for a proxy measure of sustainable competitive advantage in the form of managers' perception of their organisation's success. The causal mapping process described in Chapters 6 and 7 revealed that I was also looking at their perceptions of the factors that caused success, and at their perceptions of what was tacit and what was not.

Having weighed up the advantages and disadvantages of causal mapping, and as I have not yet come across a method that promises to be as suitable or as fruitful at eliciting tacit routines, I believe that causal

1. Introduce the process and content of the causal mapping session

2. Begin the map with success and ask the general question 'What causes success?' (A, B, C)

3. Continue the mapping process with questions such as 'What causes that?' 'How does it happen?'

4. If the flow of constructs stops, ask questions such as 'Could you give an example of how that happened?' 'Could you tell a story?'

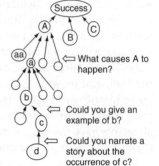

*Figure 8.1*    Researching tacit routines as a component of firms' success: summary of the refined research method (Ambrosini and Bowman, 2001a)

mapping is a worthwhile means of uncovering the idiosyncratic aspects of organisations. Figure 8.1 presents a summary of the refined method that resulted from my practical experience.

# 9
## Stage 3: Conceptual Development – Beyond Tacit Versus Explicit Organisational Knowledge

One of the findings from the mapping session at Alpha was that causal maps can reveal several types of organisational activity. In particular the session revealed not only that tacit routines matter but also that there are routines that lie outside direct management control that may also affect performance. This led me to conclude that dealing only with the basic distinction of explicit versus tacit routines is not satisfactory, and moreover that this categorisation has limited value for practising managers.

It is well documented in the management literature that there are various types of knowledge. As explained in Part I, knowledge can be tacit or objective, procedural or declarative, individual or collective, or it can be about knowing what, why, how and so on. All these categories are useful in helping us to understand what knowledge is. However in my research I discovered that they are not necessarily good at helping us to categorise all the types of routine that can be found in organisations.

What has emerged from the study on Alpha is an embryonic taxonomy that is based on these categories but extended in the light of the empirical investigation. This taxonomy is presented below. It builds on Figure 7.1, in which the concept of tacit routines was elaborated. In Chapter 7 it was explained that a routine can be tacit to one of its participants but not to another, and that a tacit routine can be either known or ignored by organisational members who do not take part in it.

### Taxonomy

Following the approach of Winter (1987), the following dimensions for routines can be proposed:

- Explicit/tacit.
- Known/unknown.
- Managers involved in routines/managers not involved in routines.
- Link with performance known/link with performance unknown.

These dimensions are explained below and illustrated with examples from the Alpha maps.

### Explicit/tacit

This basic dimension is well documented in the literature:

- Ways of doing things can be explicit – people are aware of what they are doing (for example everybody knows that they invoice everything they do).
- Ways of doing things can be tacit – people are doing things but they do them automatically and without consciously thinking about them. An activity is tacit if, prior to the research investigation, the people involved in this activity have never described or discussed it (for example managers have never realised they do not take a strictly commercial view when dealing with clients).

### Known/unknown

This second dimension is about knowing or not knowing what is happening:

- Routines may be explicitly or tacitly known – people can either describe the routines readily or they cannot do so, but they perform the routines and can recall them 'in the doing'.
- Routines may be unknown in that people are completely unaware that they are being performed. This is ignorance of the activity (for example a manager may not know how his company's multi-employer scheme works) and not evidence of a tacit routine.

### Managers involved in routines/managers not involved in routines

This third dimension is about involvement:

- Managers may be directly involved in routines, they are the performers of the routine (for example a business development director interviews potential sales employees).
- Managers may not be involved in the routines (for example a deputy CEO does not interview prospective employees).

A manager who is not involved in routines either knows or does not know about these routines. In order to know an activity tacitly an individual must be involved in it. This is related to the definition of tacit knowledge explained in Chapters 2 and 4. It is about *doing*, and not about knowing.

### Link with performance known/link with performance unknown

The fourth dimension is about linking routines to performance:

- Routines may be known and their impact on performance is also known (for example everybody knows that signing up large clients is important for the organisation's success).
- Routines may be known but it is not known that they have a positive impact on performance (for example the business director usually hires young, single people – everybody knows that, but nobody has realised that this is one of the reasons for the success of the organisation).

## Managed and unmanaged routines

The above taxonomy of organisational routines, which was developed on the basis of the causal mapping sessions, shows that there are different types of routine in organisations. This taxonomy is not only relevant theoretically but also has managerial implications. In particular it raises questions about the management of routines. Put simply, a routine is either managed or unmanaged. To explain this further we shall draw on the dimensions set out above and consider one activity with just one manager.

- *Actively managed routines* If an activity is known to happen by the manager (irrespective of whether or not he or she is involved in it) and is known to be important to performance, the routine can be actively managed. It can be changed, or deliberately left as it is. Managing an activity does not imply interfering in that activity, and if the way it is operated is allowed to continue without managerial interference this does not mean that the activity is not managed. The activity may be allowed to continue because it has been understood and recognised as valuable as it is, and the managerial tactic here is deliberate *laissez-faire*. In this case the activity is actively managed in the sense that it is deliberately left alone. An example from Alpha of such a routine is 'The frequency with which employees speak to the clients is planned and monitored'.

- *Passively managed routines* The above activity could also be passively managed, that is, left as it is not by choice but because the manager does not fully understand how it works. The manager knows that the routine is important, but does not comprehend the whole situation, only parts of it. For example not all the components of the activity are well known, or the relationship between the routine and the firm's performance is not thoroughly understood. For instance the management team at Alpha knew the adoption of management practices that embodied the best of both commercial and private practices was a key to Alpha's success, but they were not sure how this was achieved.
- *Unmanaged routines* An activity that is ignored by the manager because she or he is unaware of its existence is unmanaged and left to the devices of the doers. For instance Alpha employees went to work on Saturdays of their own accord, and some on the senior management team were unaware of this.

In summary, activities that cause success can be classified as follows:

- An actively managed routine is one that is known and understood by a manager. The manager can change the routine or leave it as it is if he or she deems it necessary to do so.
- A passively managed routine is one that is known by the manager, but she or he does not understand its ins and outs and hence it is left alone.
- An unmanaged routine is one that is left to happen because the manager does not know of its existence.

## Coding categories

When working with the management team at Alpha I concentrated on eliciting tacit routines, and subsequently the participants were asked to code the causal maps produced during the session. As explained earlier, these coding categories were:

- A: Routines that are well known to you.
- B: Routines that are known about but that you find difficult to deal with.
- C: Routines that were tacit to you until the group session.

These categories are a useful means of determining whether routines are tacit or explicit, but they are less helpful when examining other issues, such as ignorance, the passively managed and the unmanaged.

Consequently the initial coding categories need to be extended. Following the taxonomy just presented, the categories should include A (explicit routines) and C (tacit routines), plus the following:

- Routines you did not know about (this category was suggested earlier when dealing with the methodological lessons learnt from Alpha).
- Routines that you knew happened but did not realise that they mattered in terms of success.
- Routines you know are taking place but are just left to happen because they are not understood.
- Other: Activities that do not fit any of the above categories.

## Conclusion

The Alpha study showed that tacit activities – that is, organisational tacit knowledge – can be identified. However, tacit routines are not the only routines that play a crucial role in organisations. In order to deal with these routines we need not only to identify them but also to understand them. The taxonomy proposed above is a step towards doing so as it facilitates a better understanding of the complexity of routines.

# 10

# Stage 4a: Exploring Success-Generating Routines

The study conducted at Alpha revealed that tacit routines can be researched in the field using causal mapping, and that managers perceived that they could be a component of their firm's success. The study also showed that routines that lie outside direct management knowledge and control, whether tacit or not, may matter a great deal for the organisation (the passively managed and unmanaged routines discussed in the previous chapter). This particular finding is interesting from both an academic and a managerial perspective. From the managerial viewpoint, it shows how vital it is for top managers to understand fully how their organisation works if they are to sustain its success, as factors beyond their immediate concern can be of prime importance. From an academic perspective, it reveals that there is a need for a better understanding of the different types of routine that take place in organisations.

For these reasons the issue of passively managed and unmanaged activities should be examined further. The taxonomy of routines set out in Chapter 9 is a starting point, but further empirical research is necessary. For this purpose I conducted three studies. The first of these was exploratory and aimed at checking whether the finding obtained from the Alpha study – the potential importance of passively managed and unmanaged activities in success generation – was particular to that organisation. The second and third replicated the study carried out at Alpha but also took into consideration the subsequent conclusions. To a certain extent this signified that I had converted 'theory-testing research into theory building research by taking advantage of serendipitous findings' (Eisenhardt, 1989, p. 536). In this particular case, the theory-testing research into whether tacit routines could be perceived as a source of a firm's success turned into research into unmanaged routines. The first two studies are discussed in this chapter, and the third in Chapter 11.

## Omega

In order to check whether passively managed and unmanaged routines were specific to Alpha I undertook some exploratory research with managers at a British plastic-equipment manufacturing company ('Omega'). The process used for this study diverged from that used at Alpha in that:

- The managers were not interviewed prior to the mapping exercise. Before starting the mapping the managers were asked to think of a specific customer in each market they served, to list the possible reasons why these customers had chosen their company, and to note how their performance in these reasons for success compared with that of their competitors.
- The mapping process started with the factors that the managers thought Omega was better at than its competitors. The participants had not been asked to concentrate on routines when they were first briefed, but were encouraged to do so during the session.
- Once the maps were drawn the managers were not asked to code them, but I did ask them for their thoughts, on the process and content of the causal mapping session.

### Findings of the Omega study

When the Omega managers were asked what they had learnt about the causes of success in their company they first said that they now realised that this depended very much on the market in question. For instance they had become more aware that their export market was very different from their domestic market. The export market was very product-focused, and success was based on selling one patented product to a limited number of customers, and tailoring this product to these customers' various needs. The domestic market, on the other hand, was customer-focused. The success there came from providing continual support that exceeded their customers' expectations, and from having a respected brand name, being flexible and providing a high-quality, continually updated range of products. They also suggested that Omega's success had something to do with the attitudes, behaviours and philosophy that existed in the organisation, including:

- 'Having pride in our work.'
- 'Being ambitious and never satisfied.'
- 'Having contemporary thinking.'

- 'Being a small company with big ideas.'
- 'Being open to external influences.'

When encouraged to examine the maps further and to put into a few words what they meant, they came up with the metaphor of 'the company as a living organism', that what mattered was how things were interconnected. However they did not understand how these connections worked, how they had come about, and which were beneficial and which were not. In their own words, 'it was subliminal'.

Possibly the most fascinating thing to emerge in the discussion was the senior managers' genuine surprise about some of the factors that were mapped. Some of the procedures were obviously against company policy, although the participants had thought that they were authorised procedures. Who had authorised them? None of the senior managers knew and proposed that they had never actually been authorised, they had just happened and nobody had attempted to do anything about it. This discussion led the participants to conclude that it was all right to break the rules if it was to please the customer.

Thanks to the mapping it was revealed what flexibility really meant for Omega. Omega was very flexible in terms of what mattered for the customer, and this meant that employee discretion was a key to the firm's success. Employees were freed to do what they wanted as long as it was for the benefit of the customer. Moreover they were happy to take up ideas from wherever they came, they did not consider that they knew it all. All this had never been explicitly articulated, and therefore these aspects of Omega's culture had developed in an unmanaged way.

The Omega study therefore substantiated the finding from Alpha that among those routines which cause success in an organisation, some are passively managed or unmanaged.

## Kappa

### Background

Kappa is a management consultancy that was established in 1989 by three partners and now employs some 50 people. It is debt-free, profitable and growing. Kappa's client base includes organisations from both the private and the public sector, and its work tends to fall into the areas of strategic thinking, customer service, brand development and change management. The partners describe Kappa as operating at the point where business, marketing and human resource strategy meet.

All three managing partners took part in the causal mapping session. A newly employed consultant, Jane, whose task was to help Kappa develop its training and knowledge management, was also present, and although she only observed the session and took no part in the discussion she had instigated and organised the exercise. She believed that such a workshop would help her in her task and hence would help the partners and Kappa.

In the months prior to the workshop it had become increasingly apparent to the three managing directors that much of Kappa's success was due to them, so if one of them was to leave the company (or worse, if all of them were to leave) Kappa's future success might be jeopardised. Moreover, because none of them could take on any more work the prospect of growth was limited. To date they had operated as the company's main consultants and had not discussed with others in the company how they carried out their assignments, but they were now aware that Kappa's growth depended on delegation and on empowering junior consultants by providing them with the business development and client relationship skills enjoyed by themselves. However their ways of doing things had never been defined or articulated and therefore could not be passed on to others at Kappa. This is where the workshop came in.

## Identifying routines at Kappa

### The Premapping Process

In line with the revised guidelines set out at the end of Chapter 8, before starting the workshop the three partners were briefed on the aim of the session. Jane had already done this, but in order to make sure that the concept was clear and for us to get acquainted a little, it seemed beneficial to present my research and to explain why Kappa was likely to benefit from the workshop. The basic tenets of the resource-based view of the firm and tacit knowledge and routines were explained, and then, using Alpha as an example, the mapping process was outlined. Finally, some of the potential benefits of the session were highlighted and the partners were informed that they would be asked to code the maps.

When outlining the causal mapping process I again used the onion metaphor, explaining that by removing layer after layer of the reasons for success they should eventually arrive at the less explicit causes of success – that is, activities they would not ordinarily talk about. As with the Alpha study, they were told to focus on what they were currently doing, even if an activity was perceived as trivial or irrelevant, and not on what they believed they should be doing. They were also told that they would be encouraged to use verbs as a way of helping them to concentrate on their daily actions, and that the use of examples would greatly facilitate the process. Finally, they were told that it was vital for them to be open-minded, and that they should feel free to express themselves as they wished (Jane had already informed me that they were very comfortable with each other as they were all on an equal footing and valued each other's views).

### The Mapping Process

The map was constructed by placing self-adhesive notes on the revealed activities on very large blank sheets of paper pinned to the wall. The links between the factors were marked according to the partners' instructions. When necessary they were asked for clarification and examples.

Before starting the map in earnest the three partners decided which causes of success should be discussed first. A topic that captured everyone's attention was taking briefs so the mapping process started with this (the maps can be found in Appendix 4). The first point to emerge was that they did not accept briefs passively as they wanted to help their clients to understand their fundamental problems. Rather briefs were redefined and developed into new ones according to the client's real goal. For example an initial brief on the design of a brochure for a construction company was questioned and the client was made to discuss the relevant issues at the most fundamental level. This led to the brief being redefined, and it ended up as a project to build staff confidence in business development.

The discussion on the causes of success at Kappa centred on four topics: not taking the brief, engaging with the client, being confident, and friendly commerciality (that is, how the partners maintained or developed business contacts and relationships with people they liked, irrespective of whether or not they were likely to become clients). All these topics were linked and all derived from the discussion on briefs.

### Stories and metaphors

During the construction of the maps a number of stories were told. For instance the partners told the story of the brief for the construction company mentioned above, and of how they helped an executive car company to shape its brief and then won the bid for the contract. This illustrates how, by engaging with potential clients, Kappa 'won before it presented'.

Another story was of an interview with an awkward professor during the course of a project by one of the partners. The partner explained that he had decided to go into 'humble mode' and let the professor act as the expert. The professor spoke for 25 minutes, and by being humble, by playing the role of the 'kid wanting to learn', the partner found out about the professor as a person. This is an illustration of how to engage with people, of letting them talk in order to work out where they are coming from. By sitting back and listening the partners could find out whether people had something particularly noteworthy to say and whether they were investing as individuals. They also looked for 'fault lines' (anomalies, oddities) in the stories being told.

During the mapping session the partners also used metaphors. In particular the process of engaging with the client was likened to dancing with her or him in that it was a two-way, interactive process. This metaphor can be seen as the epitome of how metaphors can be used to express tacitness. It is similar to the exploding shed in reverse metaphor described in Chapter 6. This metaphor was also used to explain that engaging with the client was a continual process of discovery, and that this process was not one-sided. The aim of engaging with the client was to find a new way, and not to adopt the client's way automatically or to impose Kappa's ideas.

Hence the mapping process revealed the importance of engaging with clients, and the 'unpacking' of the engagement process led to the partners recognising that all the successful routines identified added up to 'friendly commerciality', which was the underlying philosophy in Kappa's approach. Furthermore their business philosophy was in fact their philosophy of life: they had faith in people, they were optimistic, and they believed in humour and in enjoying life.

### Coding categories

A few days after the session each of the partners was sent a copy of the map (which because of its size was divided into four parts – see Appendix 4) and asked to code it according to the categories presented at the end of Chapter 9, that is:

- A: routines that were tacit to you until the workshop (that is, activities in which you had been involved but had never discussed before). For instance one activity is 'dancing with the customer', have you ever expressed this before?
- B: routines you did not know about.
- C: routines you knew about but had not realised that they mattered.

- D: routines you know about but are left alone because they are not well understood.
- E: Other – please specify.

It was also stated that all activities that were well known to them (that is, explicit) should be left unmarked.

### Results and analysis

The three partners ('John', 'Jenny' and 'Peter') duly returned the coded maps. Before turning to the results of this it should be pointed out that most of the routines uncovered during the mapping session were intangible. They were about engaging with people: interacting with people, getting to know them, perceiving what mattered to them. Indeed the maps suggested that Kappa's success was largely based on the relationships the three directors established with their clients or potential clients. This is very much in line with the resource-based view of the firm's argument that competitive advantage is likely to derive from intangible resources and that as a consequence people are the key to organisations' success.

#### *Routines that were tacit until the causal mapping session*

John coded 17 per cent of the statements as tacit, Peter 92 per cent and Jenny none. Hence, as at Alpha (see Chapter 7), there was a noticeable difference in percentage terms of what was perceived as tacit. Twelve factors were coded as tacit by both Peter and John, including the following:

- 'We show clients why their brief may not work, then they tell us more.'
- 'We don't just ask questions, we make suggestions to help them see things they have not seen.'
- 'We do not ask for facts.'
- 'From the first question we know where to go next.'
- 'We have contacts with interesting people and people who find us interesting.'
- 'The nature of the environment (the brief and the behaviour of the people will differ in our office from what they would be in their own).'

These routines were about how the partners engaged with their clients, how they read them and then knew what to do next. When faced with a particular type of client, they knew how they should behave.

The discrepancy in the number of factors coded as tacit and the lack of agreement between the factors coded as tacit reinforces the finding for Alpha that the perception of tacitness is highly individual. While it could also reflect differences in interpreting the tacit category, it is worth reflecting on these differences. Prior to the session the three partners had been thinking a great deal about what they were doing as they had recently recognised that they were vital to the success of the business, and that if they left the business might decline. This meant that a fair amount of discovery had been done before the mapping session, whereas at Alpha it had principally been done during the session.

It is also important to note that Jenny and John were married and therefore would have most likely talked about work outside office hours, and they may well have discussed details that they had not discussed with anybody else. They may well have mentally rehearsed some routines during the period of introspection, and therefore coded these routines as not tacit. Their answers might have been different if the map had been constructed before they started their introspection. It is possible that Peter had not engaged in so much prior introspection, or when coding the maps he may have perceived that some of the routines were totally ingrained in him and had come so naturally that he had never discussed them.

When talking to Jane about the personalities of the three partners she had told me that John was in some respects the leader of the three. They were all on equal footing in terms of their position in the company, however it was John who had taken the issue of knowledge transfer most to heart. He was worried about Kappa's future and felt that the retirement of the partners in a few years' time could present very serious problems. John was also the most rational thinker of the three, and therefore throughout his years as a consultant he was more likely to have examined what he did and for what purpose. This could be similar to the situation at Alpha in respect of dealing with ego (see Chapter 7) – it is difficult for some people to admit that they lack control. These points may help explain why the three partners' coding results were so different.

*Routines that were known about but were not recognised as mattering, routines that were not known about, and routines that were left alone*

John coded 6 per cent of the factors as 'routines you knew about but did not realise mattered', Peter 4 per cent and Jenny none. Among those routines which were coded as such, three were common to Peter and John, including 'We have failed if we finish by dancing the client's dance or if the client dances our dance'. Similarly to the factors coded as tacit, these were about behaving in the right way, whoever the client, to secure the contract.

As far as 'routines you did not know about' was concerned, the result was unanimous and all three claimed that they had been aware of each one of the routines that were revealed. The results were similar for 'routines you know about but are left alone because they are not well understood'. Jenny and Peter did not allot any factor to this category, while John only allotted one: 'We don't double guess them'.

These results suggest that the partners knew all about what they were doing and why, and that they were very well aware of what was happening at Kappa. This is hardly surprising – they had founded the company and knew it inside out. Furthermore the organisation was still young and relatively small, the partners had been very 'hands-on' in terms of management style and company development, and 80 per cent of Kappa's contracts were due to their efforts. The partners were also self-aware individuals who had devoted time to introspection. The fact that they recognised that the business was extremely dependent on them and that they should transfer their knowledge to ensure easy succession meant they had been thinking about how the organisation worked.

At this stage it is worth mentioning that Jenny and John had each suggested another category. Jenny coded over 55 per cent of the factors as routines that 'we know about but are difficult *for others* to understand and learn'. Hence while Jenny considered that the partners knew very well what was happening at Kappa, she did not perceive that their employees were similarly aware. John's suggested category was 'routines that we consciously know about but have not been talked about with the staff'. He coded about 35 per cent of the factors as such. Strictly speaking these two categories are different (Jenny did not say that the partners had not talked about the routines or that the staff did not know about them; and John did not imply that the routines were difficult to understand), but they both dealt with the fact that what was known by the partners was not shared across the company as a whole.

It can be suggested that Jenny and John proposed these categories because they were seriously concerned about the dependency of the business on the three partners, and perhaps had become even more aware when constructing the maps that they and their activities were crucial to Kappa's performance and success. Both categories certainly reflected this concern, and particularly in respect of the staff's lack of awareness of how the partners worked and the lack of transfer of routines across the organisation.

*Explicit routines*

As mentioned earlier, when the three partners were asked to code the maps they were also told that activities that were well known to them (that is, explicit) should be left unmarked. For John 76 per cent of the routines were explicit, for Peter 3 per cent and for Jenny all of them. When looking at these scores it is worth considering the extent to which the personality and background of the three individuals affected their perception of tacitness. In this case the partners were very committed to doing the map – they had invited me to conduct the exercise and had been enthusiastic about the process all the way through, hence it is unlikely that there was much hiding the truth or protecting egos and I am confident that they coded the maps honestly. The comments made earlier about the partners' engagement in introspection applies here too, and it should also be noted that before joining Kappa, John had in turn been a production manager, an account representative in advertising and a director of strategy and planning, while Peter had been a management consultant and a researcher (mainly doing qualitative research). From this background it can be surmised that John was likely to be more rational and analytic (in the sense of trying to make sense of what was happening) than Peter. They both seemed intuitive and happy to be so, but John was more able than Peter to justify and explain why he did what he did. The situation is less clear with Jenny. She had a background in public relations, but as mentioned before she was living with John and may well have talked with him about her activities, and therefore nothing of what she was involved in was tacit to her.

## Discussion

It is argued that tacit routines are of crucial strategic importance because, unlike explicit routines, they are difficult to imitate and appropriate. Because tacit ways of doing things are difficult to identify and acquire it is proposed that their diffusion across the firm is limited and the uniqueness of the organisation is preserved. If we were to consider only the results of the coding by Peter, who perceived that most aspects of the work he was doing were tacit, then we could conclude that Kappa's source of success was unlikely to be at risk of imitation by competitors. This being said, it is worth considering the new categories presented by John and Jenny. In both categories the accent was on the staff and the extent to which they knew and understood what the partners were doing, about the transfer of routines and how problematic this transfer seemed to be (John and Jenny coded more than a third of the factors as belonging to these categories). If the theoretical argument were reversed, it could be suggested that routines that are difficult to communicate and transfer are likely to be tacit. Following this it can be argued that the factors Jenny coded as 'we know about but are difficult for others to understand and learn' were likely to have elements of tacitness; and that those coded by John as 'we consciously know about but have not been talked about with other staff' could be so too. Indeed we could surmise that the factors they knew about but had not discussed with others were left undiscussed because it was difficult to do so. Yet John and Jenny did not code these factors as tacit.

In Chapter 7, the definition of tacit routines was refined and it was emphasised that it is necessary to be clear about what is tacit to whom. In particular it was suggested that an activity can only be tacit to those involved in the routine, but that a routine may not be tacit to all those involved. The results obtained from the causal mapping at Kappa illustrate this point. It seems that Peter spent little time discussing what he did, whereas John and Jenny did do so, or at least between themselves. This suggests that at least in some circumstances (in this case a very small top management team of three, two of whom were husband and wife) that the notion of tacitness may need to be refined. Indeed if the above argument that factors that are difficult to transfer are likely to be tacit is correct, and if the factors coded by John and Jenny as 'not communicated to others' were tacit, then it can be proposed that these factors were known only to John and Jenny and that in some respects the couple were working as one and talked only to each other about what they were doing. This conclusion is based on Peter's results (who considered that most of the routines were tacit) and on the fact that a large number of factors (33) were coded as 'not communicated to others' by both Jenny and John. This means that about 60 per cent of the factors coded by Jenny as 'not communicated to others' were also coded as such by John, and that about 40 per cent of the factors John put in this category were also coded as such by Jenny. Peter coded all 33 factors as tacit, so it seems that these factors were 'tacit' to the couple as they had not talked about them with Peter or staff members. This conclusion is supported by the fact that the categories suggested by John and Jenny were written in the first person plural ('we', as in we knew . . . ) Considering that most of these factors had not been talked about by Peter and that John and Jenny had not communicated them to anybody else, then it can be deduced that 'we' related only to John and Jenny.

The outcome in practical terms of the routines classified by Peter as tacit and by John and Jenny as 'not communicated to others in the organisation' was certainly the same: these factors had not been expressed outside the three-partner team, and as such were unknown to or not understood by the Kappa staff. In the conclusion of the analysis of Alpha it was proposed that the benefit to managers of uncovering tacit routines is that it gives them a better understanding of how their organisation works, of the activities that take place and of how these might be managed. The Kappa case confirmed this point. The partners now had a list of routines that were crucial to Kappa's success but had not been communicated to others. They now had a starting point from which to work in order to reduce the firm's dependency on them.

If we look in more detail at the factors that had not been communicated across the organisation we can see that quite a few related to the partners' attitudes towards doing business. For example:

- 'It would be soul-destroying for us to do a job we were not happy with.'
- 'We do not maintain contacts for exploitative purposes.'
- 'We can walk away from a business opportunity.'
- 'We do not chase money at all costs.'

These attitudes and behaviours were deeply ingrained in the partners and were taken for granted. It was simply how they did business. One can refer here to Schein's (1985) three levels of organisational culture (see Chapter 2). It can be argued that the partners' way of doing business was based on taken-for-granted assumptions that were difficult to identify and explain. These assumptions accord with Schein's third level of culture – the invisible level.

Their way of conducting business and the fact that this way of doing business was a reason for Kappa's success could not be properly conveyed to or internalised by the staff unless they spent time interacting with the partners.

Other ways of operating that had not been conveyed to others relate to knowing how to behave towards clients or potential clients:

- 'We read the client.'
- 'We are not typical consultants. . . . We are not "going for the kill", clients are not punters, we are not like that.'
- 'A brief embodies assumptions that will need to be challenged.'
- 'We know that asking simple questions and being clear is key.'

- 'We allow clients to tell their story, we do not rush questions.'
- 'Your movements are affected by the client's and vice versa.'
- 'We don't take briefs because it is passive.'
- 'We challenge the brief, not the client.'

Yet others are about what it was they did that allowed them to engage with clients in special ways:

- 'We extrapolate from personal experience.'
- 'We draw things from books, films.'
- 'We find stories in the whole of our life.'
- 'My inspiration and ideas do not come from my professional life only.'
- 'You need different ways of thinking, this helps create stories.'

In summary, the causal mapping session was designed to elicit routines that generated success at Kappa. And while it became clear that the three partners knew how to behave in ways that brought success to their business, their way of doing things was not shared across the organisation. Others could not engage in the same way with clients and business contacts. They did not understand clients as the partners did, they did not know what really mattered for the clients, and hence for the business.

## Conclusions

First, the Kappa case confirms that facilitated group causal mapping is a practical and powerful way of revealing routines. By continually asking the participants to reflect on what they do, to explain how they carry out their activities, the participants are helped to express things they would not normally verbalise. The process is helped by asking simple questions such as 'What causes . . . ?', 'How do you . . . ?' and 'Could you give an example of . . . ?'

Second, the results of the coding show that some tacit routines can indeed be uncovered, and they corroborate the finding in the Alpha study that tacit activities are perceived by managers to be a component of their firm's success.

Third, while a few of the routines were classified as 'routines you knew about but did not realise mattered' and 'routines you know about but are left alone because they are not well understood', none were classified as 'not known'. Ignorance about and lack of understanding of what was happening at Kappa were not the crucial issues they were at Alpha and Gamma. This was perhaps to be expected as the three partners had founded the company, they knew it inside out and it was relatively small. However the lack of awareness of organisational members outside the team of three emerged as a serious issue.

If we compare the background information on Alpha and Kappa (see above and Chapter 8) we can see that they were very different in terms of age, size, environment and tasks. Although the three partners at Kappa were at the top of the company they were still a vital part of the operating core, in contrast to Alpha, where the top managers were more removed from operational issues. This suggests that situational factors, or to use Mintzberg's (1983) term 'contingency factors', can have a bearing on the types of routine that are perceived to be sources of success. In Part V we shall consider a number of propositions on situational factors and routines based on this suggestion, but before that the final case will be discussed.

# 11

## Stage 4b: Exploring Further Success-Generating Routines

'Delta' is the last case study reported on in this book. The top managers at Delta were conducting their annual strategy review and wanted help with exploring their success factors. It seemed that in some respects they were working their way through the available strategy tools. They had done a PEST analysis and a SWOT analysis, but after a meeting with a professor of strategy they realised they were not as aware of their sources of success as they had thought. I met the commercial development director a few days before the workshop in order to explain my research agenda and the process of causal mapping, as well as to learn something about Delta. Five people attended the subsequent workshop: the managing director, the director of delivery, the finance director, the training director and the commercial development director. In addition the business development director and the research and development director were present for parts of the process.

### Background

Delta, a subsidiary of a public limited company, was a leading supplier of IT software to the financial sector. It was founded in 1986 and was located in the City of London. Delta accounted for approximately 33 per cent of the group's turnover and in 1989–99 its total revenue came to £11.3 million. The company had a unique product, which in this chapter will be called 'the software'. Delta, which employed about 150 people, focused on supplying its integrated software, accounting and settlement systems to the wealth-management and investment-broking community. Its clients included a number of large retail stockbrokers and leading investment managers. The software was functionally rich and offered a highly automated, 'straight-through' processing system.

Built on modern client–server architecture, the software was also flexible and adaptable. Internet-and WAP-enabled, the system allowed authorised retail clients to make deals directly and to make inquiries about their accounts. Some 25 per cent of the private client transaction volume of the UK Stock Exchange was handled every day by means of the software.

## Identifying routines at Delta: the causal mapping session

### The premapping procedure

As at Alpha, the workshop started with a brief, informal presentation on the basic principles of the resource-based view of the firm. However at Delta the term core competence was used rather than successful routines as the top management team was familiar with this notion. This was followed by the same explanation of the mapping process given at Kappa (see Chapter 10). The team members were told that the coding categories were as follows:

- A: factors that are well known to you.
- B: factors that were tacit to you until the workshop (that is, activities you have never talked about until now).
- C: factors you did not know about.
- D: factors you knew about but had not realised were important to performance.
- E: factors you know about but are left alone because they are not understood.
- F: Other – please suggest a category.

Apart from category A, these categories were the same as those used at Kappa. While the partners at Kappa had been told to leave explicit factors (category A) uncoded, in retrospect this had not been a good choice as it was unclear whether the uncoded routines were indeed explicit or simply overlooked. In this respect Delta's directors took great care when coding the maps, unlike those at Alpha, who left a fair number of factors without comment.

### The mapping process

From the results published in its annual report it was clear that Delta's performance was good. By August 2000 its operating profits amounted £1 million, based on a revenue of £13.4 million. This represented a revenue increase of 19 per cent and a profit increase of 35 per cent compared with the previous year. Delta had been particularly successful in 1999–2000 because it had signed up new clients. The mapping started by asking the participants to concentrate on one of these new clients and why Delta had been successful with this customer. There was some debate about the meaning of success and being successful with a customer. The map started with the notion that 'Going live with the software' was what being successful meant, and then 'Winning the actual contract' was added.

The participants next considered the causes of success with a recently contracted US-based international financial service group, 'Sigma', and then how they had won the contract of a France-based share dealer, 'Phi', which wanted to expand its European operations. Finally, the participants decided to explore a more general source of success: the generation of revenues through services, which accounted for over 60 per cent of Delta's total revenue.

As with the previous workshops, the maps were constructed by placing self-adhesive notes on sheets of paper pinned to the wall. Altogether the map contained 125 success factors, and for ease of reading the map was divided into five parts (see Appendix 5):

- Going live with Sigma.
- Winning the Sigma contract.
- Omega.
- Revenues from services.
- Phi.

## Results and analysis

In order to facilitate comparisons and to remain consistent, when conducting the analysis I decided to use only those maps which had been coded by the five participants who had attended the entire mapping workshop. Four sets of coded maps were returned to me by the director of delivery, the finance director, the training director and the commercial development director. The results and analysis are presented below.

### Aggregate results

#### Factors that were tacit until the workshop

Between 21 per cent and 23 per cent of the factors revealed were perceived to be tacit by the director of delivery (DD), the finance director (FD) and the commercial development director (CDD), while the training director (TD) perceived 34 per cent to be so. Such percentage differences had also been found at Alpha and Kappa, and this confirms that the perception of tacitness is a personal matter, based on personal experiences and contexts, as we saw in Chapter 2. A few of the factors perceived as tacit by two or three of the directors are worth exploring because routines that are tacit to most are by definition routines that are not talked about and therefore may not be fully exploited, despite their being crucial to the firm's success. These factors are considered in detail later in the chapter.

### Factors that were not known about

The percentage of factors that were not known about by the participants varied considerably from participant to participant, ranging from about 2 per cent for the FD to 26 per cent for the CDD. For the other two the percentages were 16 per cent and 18 per cent. These differences are not surprising as they reflect individual differences such as length of time with the company, functional background and knowledge of the context, such as a specific customer, specific sources of success and so on. Indeed the CDD had been with the company for less than a year so it is not surprising that he knew less about what was happening or what had happened than the others, who had been working for Delta for much longer: the DD was a founding member, the TD had been with the company for about 13 years and the FD for about six years. While the TD and DD had been with Delta for approximately the same length of time their knowledge of the organisation's causes of success differed. The FD seemed to be unaware of very few of them, perhaps because his job meant that he was involved in many stages of the contracting process and hence knew a lot about how contracts were won at Delta. One could also speculate that he might not have been prepared to admit to ignorance (a situation similar to that at Alpha, when the 'ego' phenomenon was first observed). Factors that are ignored by most people need to be highlighted because otherwise they cannot be leveraged or protected from destruction. We shall return to this subject later.

### Factors that were known about but their effect on performance was not, and factors that were known about but had been left alone because they were not understood

Between 2 per cent and 10 per cent of the factors revealed were known about but until the workshop the participants had never realised that they were a cause of success. The percentages for 'factors that were known about but were left alone because they were not understood' ranged from 0 per cent to 5 per cent. As with the factors discussed above, we shall examine these two groups later.

## Conclusions from the aggregate results

The aggregate results indicate that on the whole the causes of success at Delta were not well understood. This means that some of the identified strengths that were essential to Delta's positive performance were unlikely to have been nurtured or developed in order to maintain or improve that performance.

As stated above, (a) the differences between the individual codings reinforce the idea that the perception of tacitness is person-specific, and (b) because the commercial director was a relative newcomer it is not surprising that he coded more activities as being unknown than did his colleagues. However, what is perhaps most striking is that despite having been with the company since its foundation or thereabouts, the training and delivery directors did not perceive that most of the revealed causes of success were explicit, which meant that the causes of success at Delta were not known in their entirety even by its most senior managers. Only the finance director coded over 50 per cent of the factors as explicit. The training director, who had been with the company for over 12 years, coded the greatest number of activities as tacit. This suggests that there is no clear relation between how much is known by an individual and how long he or she has been with the company. This is not entirely in accordance with the argument in Chapters 2 and 6 that factors might become tacit over time, with individuals increasingly taking what they do for granted, becoming more automatic in their activities and verbalising them less and less.

From an academic perspective, what needs to be done now is to examine the results to check whether the categories are relevant to all the maps, and to suggest explanations for the results obtained. From a managerial perspective, we need to identify tacit and ill-understood routines, and to see whether Delta's true strengths could be better grasped and managed. To this end each of the maps will be examined in turn.

## Results and analysis of the maps

### The Omega map

Omega was one of Delta's major clients. This high-profile company was the largest provider of online share-dealing services in the UK and a subsidiary of the leading 'execution only' stockbroker in the United States. A large majority of the factors elicited for this map (60–80 per cent) were coded as well known by all the respondents. The Omega map (see Appendix 5, Figure A5.3) examines the proposal that having Omega as a customer was a source of success for Delta (Omega was used as a referent because of its high profile). As most factors were coded as explicit, this suggests that the importance of having Omega on the client base was recognised. Furthermore, as very few factors were perceived as tacit the top team members not only understood the situation individually but had probably also discussed it. Nobody coded any factors as D and E (factors that were known about but their effect on performance was not, and factors that were known about but were left alone because they were not understood). This confirms the suggestion that the directors were well aware that having Omega for a client was a source of success for Delta, and it indicates that they understood how this source of success worked, and were able actively to manage it.

There was one factor that the participants either coded as unknown, disagreed about or left uncoded. This factor was 'Trevor's boss – 2 levels up – is doing the blackmailing'. (Trevor was employed by Omega to manage the relationship between Delta and Omega. The latter was 'blackmailing' Delta by emphasising how important it was to Delta and then making more and more demands. However it was not Trevor as such who was doing the blackmailing, but someone higher up the ladder.) This situation needed to be addressed for two reasons. First, the directors at Delta had to make sure that this was really happening, that the situation described on the map was indeed correct. Second, in order to avoid further problems they had to ensure that everybody at Delta who was or might be involved with Omega was fully aware of the situation and knew that dealing with Trevor's boss might require special care.

### The revenues from services map

This map (see Appendix 5, Figure A5.4) explored how revenues were generated from the provision of services (software development, training, support) to clients. For the participants, the majority of factors on this map were either tacitly or explicitly known. It is well known to the participants that mandatory services (for instance, ensuring that the software was 2000-compliant or ensuring that it keeps conforming to the financial authority rules) and getting the software up and running are sources of revenues, as customers have to pay for such services. This is perhaps one reason why the mapping of revenues from services only generated 10 factors. Another reason may be that there was clearly some unease about discussing the topic.

This unease was reflected in the coding of 'Customers are stuck once they have the product'. Only the CDD coded this as explicitly known. The TD disagreed with this coding, the DD felt that the factor was not understood and the FD perceived it as tacit. This suggests that while the people at Delta knew that the company was making money by locking in the customers, they were not entirely happy with the situation and were reluctant to discuss it. It was clear during the session that the participants had entered a zone of uncomfortable debate (Bowman, 1995).

There was some discussion about whether services were actually a source of success. The TD thought they were not because the revenues were coming from servicing software recently bought by new clients and from clients who had to keep up with mandatory changes. In other words, if the product had been right in the first place, clients would not be paying extra for these services. While the mapping continued because, as stated by the CDD, 60 per cent of Delta's revenue came from servicing its software, the debate was uneasy and there was tension in the air; the atmosphere changed. The debate mainly focused on the sustainability of this source of success.

Clients were locked in to Delta and its software because of the cost of exit. However it was argued that in the future customers might well decide to face up to the cost and time implications and abandon the software. It was also clear that some of the participants in the workshop, particularly the longer-standing directors, were uncomfortable about the fact that Delta was making money by fencing in clients and leaving them with little choice but to pay to correct bugs in the system, even if they felt they should not. In summary, the fact that revenues were generated by trapping customers was known and shared, but it was not openly discussed despite being crucial to Delta's success.

### The going live with Sigma map

The coding of this map (see Appendix 5, Figure A5.1) differed significantly from the previous ones ('going live' in this context is about the customer using the software). The most noteworthy difference was that the FD considered that 50 per cent of the factors on the map were well known; for the DD this percentage was 30 per cent and for the others 17 per cent. There was no single factor that everybody agreed was well known. This indicates that this proposed cause of success was difficult to define and discuss, and therefore, some of the factors that were perceived to be components of Delta's success with Sigma might well have been reasons for the firm's good performance as according to the resource-based view of the firm, routines that are difficult to express and explain are sources of superior performance because they are difficult to imitate by competitors. Indeed if Delta itself did not really understand its routines, it is highly unlikely that its competitors would have been able to do so. As relatively few factors were perceived to be explicit by all the participants, it is likely that some of the activities plotted on the 'Going live' map were embedded in the organisation, were specific, difficult to talk about and hence a source of sustainable success.

Fourteen of the 22 factors were coded as tacit by at least one participant. Factors that were coded as tacit by at least two participants were:

- 'We developed a software specific to them.'
- 'We win new players, new entrants to the market, rarely established organisations' (that is, Delta mainly signed up new entrants to the market and rarely obtained business from established organisations).
- 'Senior staff were actively involved in the implementation process.'

This result is in accordance with that for explicit factors and reinforces the point that the reasons for success in 'Going live with Sigma' were not well articulated or documented. This is also supported by the number of factors that were unknown to some directors – indeed over 60 per cent of the factors revealed were coded as unknown by at least one person. Two factors were completely ignored by three participants:

- 'The functionality of the software was not considered by Sigma when the decision was made to use it.'
- 'The IT team was available for advice but did not take part in the decision-making process.'

The latter factor was known about, but until the session it had not been known that it had played part in Delta's success with Sigma.

Altogether just under a quarter of the factors were perceived as either unknown, known about but not known to matter to success, or known but left alone because they were not understood. This shows that the factors that led to success with Sigma flowed from activities that were likely to be difficult to imitate by competitors because they were not even well understood by Delta's directors. It also suggests that this success was potentially vulnerable and needed to be protected.

Finally, there seemed to be some disagreement about whether there was usually little competition. This meant that either some people thought that this was the case and some did not, or that there was uncertainty at Delta about what competition meant in terms of degree or who the competitors were. This could be well worth exploring by Delta to ensure that taken-for-granted assumptions about competition do not prevent action or lead to complacency.

*Winning the Sigma contract*

The coding of this map (Appendix 5, Figure A5.2) was quite similar to that of 'Going live with Sigma'. Everybody but the FD coded the majority of factors as not explicit, not clearly known. This suggests that sustainable sources of the firm's success were included in the map.

Over 70 per cent of the factors were perceived to have been tacit until the workshop by at least one director. This meant that a very large proportion of the reasons why the contract had been won had not been articulated or discussed. It was only during the construction of the map that the various participants began to recognize this. Two factors were tacitly known by three of the participants:

- 'We had personal relationships with people at the top of Sigma.'
- 'Whenever a problem appeared we compromised.'

When the latter factor was not coded as tacit it was coded as ignored. As the two factors were tacit to the top management team they would not have been known elsewhere in the company, and notably by the sales team. By becoming aware of such factors, in future they could act on them and perhaps become more successful at winning contracts.

Another point worth mentioning is the number of factors that were unknown: over half of the causes of success were not known by at least one person. Three were unknown to all but one:

- 'The CEO of Sigma's decision was based on his feeling that the delivery manager knew what she was doing.'
- 'The CEO of Sigma never looked at the software.'
- 'For non-UK customers this is a selection – being a public organisation.'

Once again these may have significance for future sales. They show the importance of building strong personal relationships with potential customers, of knowing who one is talking to and how they make their decisions. Heavily emphasising the benefits and technical aspects of the software may have been a hindrance when dealing with a client such as Sigma, but the reverse would have been true if the customer's greatest interest had been the technical aspects of the software. Hence the sales pitch could be formulaic, and being able to adapt the pitch, knowing what to say to whom, appears to have been key to Delta's winning of the Sigma contract.

Finally, one factor was ignored by the CDD, and while it had been known to the TD and DD before the workshop they had not realised that it was a source of success: 'They did not see us as doing any hard sales'. This too was linked to the sales process, and combined with the other routines on the map it enabled Delta to win the Sigma contract.

### The Phi map

As mentioned earlier, Phi was a France-based share dealer that needed Internet broking facilities to expand its European operations. For all but the TD, most of the factors on the map (Appendix 5, Figure A5.5) were well known. Although quite a few of those linked to where the contract came from were not known, and about two thirds were known tacitly by at least one participant: 'They perceived we knew our business' was tacit to three respondents, and 'We are part of a large group' was either tacit or known, but the link with performance was not. Taken together the factors linked to Delta's size and the benefits that engendered in terms of stability and support capacity were known but had not been made explicit until the workshop. Therefore the importance of these factors to customers would not have been well known to others in the company, and hence the sales force may have been missing a vital selling point. The same applies to the software and its suitability for the Internet broker market. There were two factors that directly addressed the latter, both of which were coded as tacit by the TD and the FD, while the DD coded one of them as tacit. This suggests that this suitability to any specific customer may not have been discussed widely at Delta.

It is worth mentioning that the Phi map was the last to be drawn. It was relatively small in that it consisted of just 27 concepts. Perhaps more importantly the mapping had to be halted because some of the causes of success with Phi were not known to the participants as the routines used to win the Phi contract had not been revealed to them. Ideally the map should have been completed by those individuals who had been involved. However after a few factors had been elicited in the Phi mapping process the research and development director (R&DD) joined the workshop and proved to be of great help. It was only after he came in that the top management team were able to talk about Phi. This was an interesting situation to observe as it involved the 'Aha!' element – the exclamation prompted by something that had been tacit being made explicit. Up to that point the construction of the various maps had been very much a group process, with all being involved in the discussions on the factors, but with the Phi map the team tended to sit back and listen to the R&DD. As he spoke there was considerable laughter because almost word for word he was repeating the process that had taken place with the Sigma map, despite the fact that he had not taken part in the construction of that map. He obviously did not understand the reason for the laughter, but to me it seemed to represent 'Eureka!' Suddenly the directors were able to draw parallels between the maps, and these parallels became explicit in terms not only of the concepts elicited but also of the similarities between the two contracts.

## Discussion

As mentioned at the start of this chapter, Delta's decision to explore the causes of its success was part of a review process aimed at evaluating the strategic options available to the firm. Five maps were constructed, consisting of routines and factors that had been tacit, unknown or not well understood until the workshops. These can now be examined as a whole in order to gain further insights into the causes of success at Delta. There is little point in reiterating all the factors mentioned in the previous sections, but it will be interesting to draw parallels between the maps, to highlight recurring themes and to discuss some of the clearly successful routines that were revealed during the mapping sessions.

One of the success factors that emerged in most of the mapping sessions was Delta's ability to show that it was a stable company that would be there well into the future. The maps also indicated that customers needed reassurance, and Delta's ability to provide such reassurance was a definite component of its success. The following were elements of these factors.

- Because Delta belonged to a Plc it had to publish its accounts, and hence its performance could be scrutinised.
- Because it belonged to a Plc it was stable and could be trusted.
- Delta was large in terms of staff (in comparison with its competitors) and therefore could provide support.
- Because Delta had only one product it would not neglect it.

Moreover having Omega as a customer could certainly be added to this list. Being able to demonstrate that such a respected company used the Delta software showed that Delta was trusted by Omega and served to reassure other customers.

Looking at the coding results set out in this chapter, the fact that Delta benefited from being able to reassure its customers did not seem to have been widely recognised. Some elements of this were known, but not all of them and therefore it can be suggested that reassurance as a source of success was not clearly comprehended, was not explicitly communicated throughout the company and had not been properly exploited. Routines are about actions, about interrelating with people and tangible resources. In particular tacit routines, as we saw in Chapters 2 to 4, are about doing things, for instance exploiting, combining and selecting resources in a non-prescribed way that has not been talked about. Reassurance is provided through inert objects such as software or the annual report, but the ways in which the act of providing reassurance is translated into a source of success is not well understood.

Another success factor at Delta was 'Having a business approach rather than an IT approach'. This appears to have been context-specific, that is, the maps indicate that it was valuable when serving 'traditional' businesses such as Sigma but not Internet users such as Phi. However the maps did not cover all Delta's customers and therefore this needs to be checked.

Negotiating at the top level also seemed to be a key success factor. This allowed Delta to build up trust by having top managers talk to its customers about their strategies, by not 'hard' selling and showing that it wanted to understand their business needs in order to meet them. It was ready to compromise, to marry the customer's needs to its own. This business-oriented rather than technical approach was clearly a source of success, as indicated by elements on the maps that related to relationships at the top level and their understanding of business models. It was also indicated by factors that related to the lesser role played by the product, such as 'Customers did not look at the product' and 'The IT team was available for advice but did not take part in the decision-making process'.

Another cause of success revealed by drawing parallels between the Sigma and Phi maps was Delta's ability to 'Adapt the sales pitch to the customer' or 'Match the pitch to the customer'. Sigma needed a business-oriented approach whereas Phi needed a technical one, and each received what it wanted. This successful routine was about Delta's ability to identify the required emphasis (on the software or on business issues) and being able to deliver it. It also suggests that the ability to sense the right approach early in the engagement was vital to building up the relationship.

'Providing reassurance to customers' and 'Having a business approach rather than an IT approach' were the two success routines that emerged most clearly from the workshop. Obviously they were not the only ones, but only some parts of the company were mapped and this was done in a very limited time period.

With regard to the Phi map, it emerged that the software (and possibly the Internet market in general) was a major reason for success. However this did not constitute a routine, a way of doing things that was not prescribed or talked about. Rather it was a tangible product. The maps did not reveal any special routines embedded in the software, or in the use of the software by Delta. For instance nothing about innovation, research or team skills was mentioned, but in order to develop the software and turn it into a market leader they must have existed in the past. However, the fact that the software was a unique product but was being sold only to a limited market indicates that these skills had not been recognised and exploited, and might even have been lost. While the resource-based view of the firm argues that a product is highly unlikely to be a source of *sustainable* competitive advantage, at that point Delta's product still had little competition and once they possessed the software, customers were somewhat locked in. The complexity of the software's architecture not only prevented customers from fully understanding the product, but also made it difficult for competitors to reverse engineer and imitate it.

Routines that are sources of sustainable competitive advantage are history-dependent. They are based, among others, on particular employees and past investments. Discovering and repeating the development processes that resulted in the software would be impossible for competitors. However in the absence of further refinement of the product, competitors eventually unlock its secrets (Dierickx and Cool, 1989). Hence Delta's top management team needed to recognise that the software might not be a market leader forever and that its future life might be limited.

Returning to the 'Revenues from services' map, as we saw in the previous section, locking in clients with costly and complex barriers to exit and then making them pay for the software to be serviced was a source of revenue that the participants at Delta were reluctant to discuss, making it vulnerable to changes of staff. For example a new product manager or CEO who was unaware of the situation might ask for the product to be scrutinised and improved, and hence the revenue stream might dry up. In short, if the software was made fail-proof, worked perfectly well and was very easy to use, such improvements, as rational as they might seem ('We want to sell a perfect product') would jeopardise Delta's main source of income.

At the mapping session, because the topic was seemingly taboo for the long-serving managers, only a newcomer could address the issue properly. This was what happened with the CDD, who was unaware of the sensitivity of this ethical issue (the customers' dependence is being exploited). Furthermore he did not have the same emotional attachment to the software because he had not been involved in its development and had not lived with it for the past 14 years. This was not the case with the TD and the DD, who referred instead to the 'good old days' when 'we did not think of making money, we just wanted to develop a good product, the best product'.

At this point it is worth returning to the start of the mapping process and the discussion on what success meant at Delta. We have seen that there were three views on the meaning of success: 'going live' with the software, winning the contract, and generating revenues from services. These three sources of success were all agreed upon, but each had its own champion. For the CEO success was mainly about winning contracts, for the TD it was about going live with the software, and for the CDD it was mainly about generating revenues from services. These differences reflected their functions in the firm, and perhaps also their attitudes and length of service. For the CEO it was all about clinching deals and adding to the client base, which showed that the software was still in demand. The CDD had not been with Delta for long, so for him Delta's main source of success was what brought in Delta the most revenue – service provision. He was also in charge of planning and analysing the company's position, 'the numbers game'. For the TD, success came when customers started to use the product and experience it. He was proud when clients recognised the value of the product he had worked on for the past 13 years.

## Conclusions

The first conclusion to be drawn is the same as one drawn for Alpha and Kappa; causal mapping is a powerful technique for surfacing routines, including ones that are tacit, ignored or not well understood. The process of causal mapping prompts participants to suggest reasons for their firm's success and enables them to move progressively closer to the heart of the matter. At Delta the questions asked included: 'How did it happen?' 'How did Delta . . . ?' 'Where did this come from?' 'How do you get . . . ?' The task of mapping was relatively simple and non-threatening. With all the teams the atmosphere was relaxed, the participants knew they were not being assessed and they wanted the mapping to take place, but at the same time they were challenged by being asked to dig deeper and deeper for the reasons for Delta's success. As the facilitator was in charge of writing down the participants' suggestions on the self-adhesive stickers, the participants were compelled to explain what they meant and avoid jargon, and because the facilitator controlled the flow of the map, clarifications could be easily asked for.

The maps constructed with Delta's top management team revealed several causes of Delta's success, and showed that a number of the factors in its success were not well known or discussed. Once these had been identified, the team could start working on Delta's new strategic direction with greater confidence. In particular the maps gave them some understanding of which factors needed to be maintained and protected, and which could be developed and perhaps transferred throughout Delta or the organisation as a whole. Questions that the managers may want to raise include the following. 'Are our routines continuously improved and enhanced?' 'Are they shared across the organisation, and notably the sales team?' 'Does the sales team know about the importance of adapting the pitch to the customer?' 'Does Delta know how to deal with Trevor's bosses in order to keep Omega as a good customer, and hence as a selling point?' We shall return to these questions in Part V, but first we shall look at some of the lessons drawn from the Delta and Kappa cases.

# 12
# Stage 5: Conclusions Drawn from the Mapping Sessions at Kappa and Delta

The Alpha case showed that routines that were tacit to managers could be elicited by means of causal mapping and that managers could connect these routines to their firm's success. When reporting the case, it was stated that one consequence of mapping Alpha's causes of success was the realisation that while tacit routines may indeed be valuable, a range of other routines that are not well documented in the literature also play a part in positive performance. Hence mapping sessions were conducted at Omega, Kappa and Delta to examine whether the findings from the Alpha study were also relevant to other organisations. It emerged that these findings could be applied to other cases, and that other valuable routines could be identified.

The studies have given us a better understanding of what occurs in the 'black box' of the firm. It turns out that the box is almost as black when viewed inside the firm as it is from the outside. Some success-generating routines are well known, but some are far from transparent to the top management team and therefore it may be even more difficult for competitors to unscramble reasons for the firm's success.

Chapters 10 and 11 analysed the causal maps constructed by the partners at Kappa and by Delta's senior managers. The contents of each of these maps were commented upon. For instance it was pointed out that the routines that were perceived to be key components of Kappa's success reflected the partners' beliefs about how business should be conducted, how they should engage with clients and how personal experiences could enrich the conducting of business. This meant that if they were to reduce the dependency of the business on their own input before they retired they had to pass on to the staff their knowledge, the nature of their routines, the way in which they interacted with clients and how they utilised personal experiences.

Figures 12.1 and 12.2 illustrate the types of routine that were revealed at the Kappa mapping session.

In terms of the key components of Delta's success, three of the main success-generating factors perceived by the managers were:

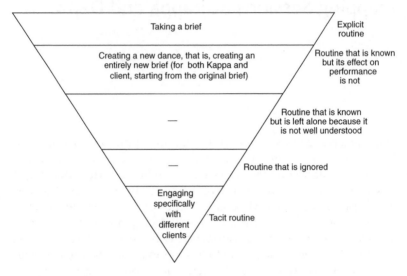

*Figure 12.1*    Routines at Kappa: 'taking a brief'

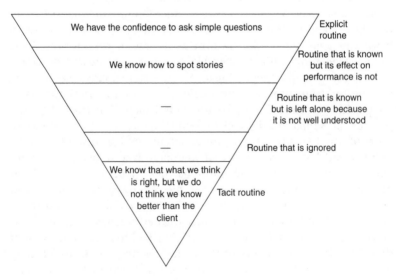

*Figure 12.2*    Routines at Kappa: 'displaying confidence'

- 'Providing reassurance to customers.'
- 'Having a business approach rather than an IT approach when dealing with traditional businesses.'
- 'Adapting the sales pitch to the customer.'

Figures 12.3–5 illustrate the types of routine that relate to each of these.

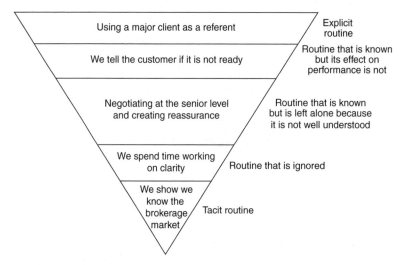

*Figure 12.3*   Routines at Delta: 'providing reassurance to customers'

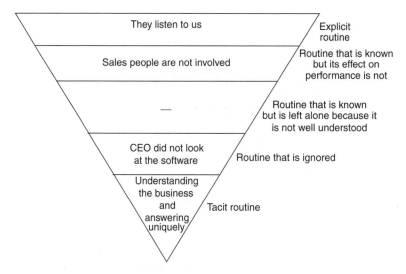

*Figure 12.4*   Routines at Delta: 'a business approach, not an IT approach'

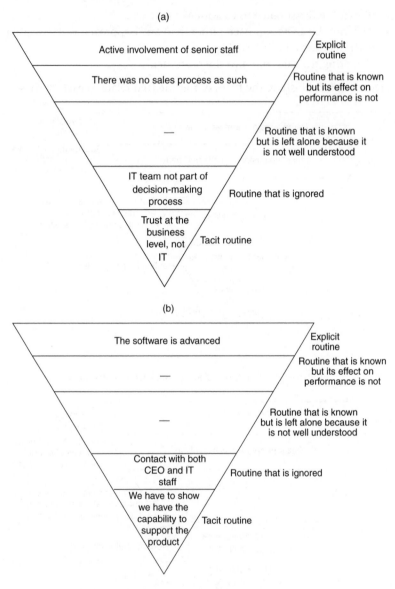

*Figure 12.5*    Routines at Delta: 'adapting the sales pitch to the customer'. (a) Sigma, a traditional broker; (b) Phi, an internet broker

The pie charts in Figure 12.6 show the percentage of routines that were coded by the participants as explicit, tacit, ignored, known

The Phi map

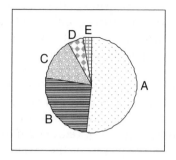

'Winning the Sigma contract'                'Going Live with Sigma'

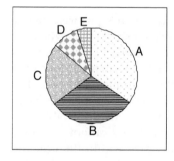    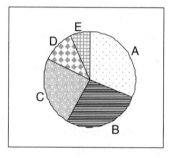

A: Explicit routines
B: Tacit routines
C: Routines that are ignored
D: Routines that are known about but their effect on performance is not
E: Routines that are known but are left alone because they are not well understood

*Figure 12.6*  Comparison of the codings for the maps on Phi, 'Winning the Sigma contract' and 'Going live with Sigma'

but not known that they were linked to performance, or not well understood.

As can be seen, there is a clear difference between the Phi map and those for Sigma. For the Phi map, 50 per cent of the routines were coded as A, 25 per cent as B, 14 per cent as C, 5 per cent as D and 3 per cent as E. For the 'Winning the Sigma contract' map 34 per cent of the routines were coded as A, 39 per cent as B, 21 per cent as C, 9 per cent as D and 5 per cent as E. For the 'Going live with Sigma' map, 31 per cent of the routines were coded as A, 27 per cent as B, 24 per cent as C,

11 per cent as D and 7 per cent as E. On the whole there was a clear understanding among the participants of the reasons for Delta's success with Phi, and three of the four participants coded over 50 per cent of the factors as explicit. Hence fewer activities were perceived as tacit or not well understood than was the case with the activities revealed for the Sigma maps.

The Phi results can be interpreted as relating to Delta's ability to adapt its sales pitch to the customer. As discussed in the previous chapter, Delta was successful with Phi because it convinced the latter that the software was technologically advanced, multifunctional, internet friendly and used by the key players in the execution-only brokerage market. All these factors were tangible, easy to understand and did not require special selling skills other than the ability to convey the right information to the potential customer.

Conversely the key factors in Delta's success with Sigma were mainly intangible, such as 'We had a personal relationship', and 'Whenever a problem appeared we compromised'. These approaches were not covered by rules laid down in manuals and therefore were more difficult to deal with than tangible resources or codified information. Hence they were less easy to describe and codify than the causes of success with Phi.

As mentioned in Part I, a firm's success depends on its ability to protect difficult-to-imitate routines. These routines cannot be readily traded, and they are likely to have been created within the firm and hence are context-specific, taken for granted, tacit or not well understood, and may be nearly impossible to transfer to different contexts (Teece, 2000). Such routines were characteristic of those revealed by the Delta managers when mapping their reasons for Delta's success with Sigma.

The differences between the types of routine revealed for Phi and Sigma suggest that the causes of success could not be managed similarly in both cases. Based on the issues raised in Chapter 9 about the management of routines, (section entitled 'Managed and unmanaged routines') it could be hypothesised that the routines that accounted for the success with Phi were likely to have been actively managed and those for Sigma passively managed. In Chapter 9 it was proposed that managers can manage routines in three fashions: they can actively manage them, passively manage them or leave them unmanaged.

At Phi and Omega, as we saw in the previous chapters, many of the factors that were perceived to account for Delta's success were known to happen and known to matter in terms of performance. This means that, based on the three dimensions set out in Chapter 9, they can be actively managed. They can be changed or deliberately left as they are (as managing an activity does not imply interfering in it) because they are recognised as being valuable in their present form. All the factors coded as explicit by most of the Delta managers were likely to have been actively managed (including contributors to success that were not routines as such). For example:

- 'Omega is used as a reference.'
- 'Our client base.'
- 'The software is technologically advanced.'
- 'Lots of time was spent before the contract was signed.'
- 'The size of Delta matters.'

It is worth remembering, though, that such factors can be imitated in their effects by competitors, for example competitors will have their own referent clients. Very often these factors are tangible and understandable to competitors. This means that while they are valuable they are unlikely to be a sustainable source of profits as they are not unique or difficult to imitate, and can be substituted for.

However a tacit or not well understood routine is very difficult to copy as those who engage in it are not readily able to express what they are doing. Nonetheless their managers may clearly know about it, in which case they have a potential jewel in their hands. Here management action can be either detrimental in the long term or beneficial. By knowing a tacit routine managers are able to codify it and thereby transform it into an explicit routine. This makes it more manageable, but it may equally cause it to lose its capacity to be a sustainable source of profits. However by virtue of their knowledge of tacit or not well understood routines they can ensure that the routines are protected and thereby, as long as the environment remains more or less the same, preserve this source of success.

The routines that Delta's managers coded as tacit or not well understood could only, as argued in Chapter 9, be passively managed (that is, left alone, without any intervention), not by choice but because they did not understood how these routines worked. They did not comprehend the whole situation, only parts of it. For instance they might not have understood all the components of a success factor, or the interrelationship between the factor and performance was not thoroughly understood. Factors that were coded by some managers as those which were left alone because they were not well understood were 'We positioned ourselves as a partner, not only as a product provider', and 'They did not see us doing any hard selling'. Managerial action in this case would be limited by the fact that it is difficult to leverage what is not well understood. However at least the managers could protect the success-creating activity.

Finally, routines that are ignored by managers can only be left unmanaged, that is, left to the devices of those involved in the activity. The danger here is that managers might inadvertently destroy a routine that is valuable, for instance during the process of downsizing, cost cutting and so on. Moreover their ignorance of the routine means that they are unable not only to protect it but also to develop it. Obviously, because maps are coded by those who construct them no factor can be unknown to all. However there are factors that are unknown to most and if the person who understands them is not in charge of managing them they remain unmanaged and vulnerable. Examples from the Delta study of managers not knowing the details of their company's operations are:

- 'The CEO of Sigma never looked at the software.'
- 'For non-UK customers this is a selection factor – public versus non public organisation.'
- 'The functionality of the software did not figure in Sigma's decision to use Delta.'
- 'The IT team was available for advice but did not take part in the decision-making process.'

For factors coded as known but the link with performance is not, despite being passively managed the consequences are similar to those for factors that are ignored as it is problematic to manage something whose outcomes or effects are unknown. This is also the case with tacit routines when the managers of these routines do not know about them. There are no examples of this for Delta as the maps were not constructed by staff at different functional levels.

As discussed at the end of the previous chapter, the maps constructed during the workshop revealed that there were numerous causes of Delta's success and that a number of valuable routines were not well known or discussed. Once these had been identified the managers could begin to consider future changes. Questions that might be addressed include the following. Are the routines capable of being continuously improved and enhanced? Are they shared across the organisation, and notably by the sales team? Does the sales team know about the importance of adapting the pitch to the customer? Does Delta know how to deal with Trevor's bosses in order to keep Omega as a good customer, and hence as a selling point? Are there any new market opportunities in which the current routines could be used? Are there markets that share the same context?

The identification of current routines can reveal that new competences need to be addressed, such as does Delta need new competences in order to exploit its current market? Are there any new market opportunities, and does Delta have appropriate routines to exploit them?

Finally, more general issues can be raised by the maps. Who are Delta's competitors? How strong is the competition? (This issue was raised when discussing the Phi contract.) What are the causes of the managers' problem with discussing revenues from services? What is Delta's philosophy? Is it business-oriented or technically oriented? A technical orientation may imply that Delta should keep developing the software in order to make it better and better, whereas a less technical orientation could suggest selling and servicing a software that fulfils a limited set of purposes.

These managerial implications and the theoretical implications from the case studies are developed in the following chapters, which will also consider more general implications and possible developments from the research. The next two sections of this chapter summarise some conclusions drawn from the literature and the empirical research with Alpha, Delta and Kappa, and consider specific developments that could be inferred from the latter two cases.

## Consolidation

This section discusses a few points from the literature, plus lessons that were learnt from the Alpha study and supported by the Delta and Kappa studies.

First, causal mapping is a practical way of revealing success-generating routines, including tacit routines. In particular it appears to be a useful means of enabling participants to reflect on what has a positive impact on their organisation's performance. As routines emerge and are discussed, the participants' memories are jogged and items surface that they would normally be unable to recall.

Second, the case studies have shown that a routine may not be tacit to all those involved (see Chapter 7, Figure 7.1). This suggests that attention should be paid to what is tacit to whom, and that coding should be done by each individual and not the group as a whole. In the same vein a single routine could perhaps be broken down (further than was done in the maps) into numerous elements, with some being tacit and others explicit.

Third, the case studies confirm the common argument that what is vital to an organisation's performance is not what is laid out in its accounts. What is described in the balance sheet is likely to give a poor picture of a firm as it is static. Two organisations with the same list of assets might perform very differently simply because of their differing use of these assets and their differing organisational routines.

Finally, the case studies show that the coding categories are meaningful to most managers. In particular they support the proposition that routines that are ignored by some managers or are not well understood might play a crucial role in an organisation.

## Development

To a large extent the Delta and Kappa studies confirmed the results obtained at Alpha, and they also revealed a few new aspects that may be worth mentioning before embarking on some more general implications.

One of the lessons learnt from the Delta and Kappa studies is that it would be beneficial to add further coding categories to those already in use. In particular the coding categories could be modified and some new ones added to suit the organisation undergoing the mapping process, and to refine our knowledge of routines. The two studies suggest that the following categories would be useful:

- Routines that are known but not communicated or transferred to others.
- Routines that are known by some but others do not understand.
- Routines that are known about but are not discussed because they involve a taboo subject.
- Routines people do not know about but do know where to obtain information on them.
- Routines people know they do not know much about (for example they have never been involved in a particular contract negotiation process but knew it happened).

The first two categories could prompt organisations to investigate whether valuable routines could be shared across the organisation if they were explained or taught to other organisational members.

The third category is about routines that people are aware are going on but are not readily talked about because it is uncomfortable to do so. They are routines that generate tension, emotional discomfort and criticisms when talked about, so are not usually discussed. They are virtually ignored in terms of being managed as nobody dares to do anything about them.

The last two are about ignorance. Ignorance is an issue in itself, but in terms of understanding how managers act in respect of valuable routines it would be useful to determine whether they are simply ignoring a routine or do not know about it, and if they are ignoring it, whether they know where to obtain information on it.

The case studies also show that success can have numerous causes, and that when investigating what makes a particular firm outperform another one cannot expect just a single reason to be given. The studies also highlight that not all success factors are well known across the organisation. Hence it cannot be assumed that all valuable routines are being deliberately managed. There is a need to be specific about the causes of success that are being discussed.

The following chapters move away from empirical research and consider the more general theoretical and managerial implications of the studies.

# Part V

# Implications and Conclusions

# 13
# Theoretical Contributions

This last part of the book focuses on the conclusions and implications that can be drawn from the previous chapters. This chapter is dedicated to methodological and theoretical developments and the next to managerial implications. The aim is not to reiterate what has been argued before, but to summarise the potential contributions to the field of strategic management and tacit knowledge that were set out earlier, and to point out others that stem from the empirical and literature review elements of the book.

## Methodological contributions

### Defining tacit knowledge as an empirically researchable concept

Having demonstrated in the literature review that tacit knowledge is an important phenomenon to study (Grant, 1993; Spender, 1994) but that the subject has remained theoretical and little empirical evidence has been published (Jensen, 1993; Rao, 1994), the next task was to clarify and operationalise the concept of tacit knowledge, because 'if a construct is conceptually clear but empirically impossible to measure, then it is of limited utility in advancing our quest for knowledge' (Thomas and Pollock, 1999, p. 137).

In Parts I and II the concept of tacit knowledge was explained and clarified in order to find avenues to operationalise the concept. A distinction was drawn between individual tacit knowledge, which I call tacit skills, and organisational tacit knowledge, which I call tacit routines. These distinctions help to emphasise that tacit knowledge is not about knowing in the abstract, it is about action, about doing. Being able to define tacit knowledge as tacit routines and specify that they are non-prescribed ways of doing things in an organisation that have not yet been articulated was the first outcome of the research reported here.

### Methodology for empirically researching tacit routines

As noted earlier, despite widespread agreement that tacit routines play a crucial part in generating sustainable competitive advantage there has been little empirical research to support this argument. This is due to the challenges that empirically examining tacit routines entail, especially finding a way of uncovering what people are involved in but cannot readily talk about.

By defining tacit knowledge as tacit routines and reviewing the methodologies used to study intangible phenomena it was possible to design a methodology for studying tacit routines in the field. Group mapping of the perceived causes of organisational success, followed by individual coding has proved a powerful way of eliciting tacit ways of doing things that have a positive impact on organisational perform-ance. This technique is effective because it allows participants to reflect on what they do when carrying out their work, and to verbalise for the first time the nature of what it is they do that causes success in the organisation. The case studies have proved that the chosen research strategy is indeed an effective means of uncovering tacit activities. In other words the research has shown that tacit routines can be researched in the field, and that they may be perceived by managers to be a component of their firm's success (Ambrosini and Bowman, 1997, 1999, 2000).

Thus a new research strategy that allows tacit routines to be empiric-ally studied was the second main outcome of the research reported here. The next was the ability to provide examples of situations where tacit routines had been perceived as crucial to organisational performance. The claim can therefore be made that this study has provided empirical support to the argument that tacit routines can be a source of competi-tive advantage.

## Theoretical developments

### Elaboration of the concept

The concept of tacit knowledge has been clarified thanks to this research. As recalled above, tacit knowledge has been divided into tacit skills and tacit routines. It has also been shown that there are degrees of tacitness (Chapter 4), and that when dealing with tacit routines (that is, organisational tacit knowledge) one needs to specify to whom they are tacit, as the same routines may be explicit to some and tacit to others in the organisation (Chapter 8).

## Valuable routines

*Ignorance and causal ambiguity*

One of the findings of the case studies was that while tacit routines play a part in organisational success, other types of routine clearly contribute as well. Explicit routines can also be linked to success as despite the fact that they are vulnerable to imitation they are sources of competitive parity (Barney, 1995). They may only be prerequisites – they are order-qualifying rather than order-winning criteria – but they are essential if the firm is to be able to compete in its industry.

The studies have also shown that tacitness should not be confused with ignorance, that there are routines that are known to exist but not that they effect success, and that there are routines that are left as they are because they are not understood. The two latter types of routine can be related to causal ambiguity.

In Chapter 1 causal ambiguity – ambiguity between actions and results – was described as an isolating mechanism that protects the firm from competitive imitation, and it was argued that tacitness is one of the main sources of causal ambiguity. In a recent paper Wilcox King and Zeithaml (2001) made a distinction between linkage causal ambiguity and characteristic causal ambiguity. They define linkage ambiguity as 'ambiguity among decision makers about the link between competency and competitive advantage' and characteristic ambiguity as 'ambiguity inherent to the resource itself' (ibid., p. 77), with tacitness being the main generator of characteristic ambiguity. The coding categories used in the present research to analyse the causal maps can be associated with these two types of ambiguity. 'Routines that were tacit until the workshop' and 'routines that are known about but left alone because they are not well understood' are about characteristic ambiguity; while 'routines that were known about but the fact that they mattered was not' are about linkage ambiguity.

As the results of the coding have shown, instances of both types of ambiguity were identified in the case studies, and this also represents a contribution to the field as it addresses 'the need to examine how a firm actually experiences causal ambiguity' (Mosakowski, 1997, p. 438).

The studies have also allowed the subject of ambiguity to be developed further. In particular they have shown that ignorance – not knowing about what is happening – is a separate factor from causal ambiguity. Causal ambiguity relates to situations where the link between action and result is not known. It does not relate to situations where nothing is known. This is important as ignorance seems not to have been dealt with by many researchers, despite the fact that managers' ignorance of what is happening in their firm is likely to have many strategic implications. We shall return to this issue later.

Another development concerns who knows what. Earlier it was recalled that a routine may be tacit to some but not to others. This can now be expanded: a routine may be causally ambiguous to some but not to others. In terms of strategy, it is of relevance to distinguish between causal ambiguity perceived by the *performer* of a routine and causal ambiguity perceived by the *managers* of the performers of the routine. According to the definition of tacitness a routine can only be tacit to somebody involved in it, to those who perform it, and this argument can be extended to ignorance of success-generating routines: a routine can only be ignored by somebody who is not involved in it. With this established one can better apprehend the management of routines (Chapter 9) and highlight situations in which a routine is likely to be actively managed, passively managed or unmanaged.

### Ignorance, causal ambiguity and the management of routines

It could be argued that the following discussion is as much about managerial implications as it is about theoretical implications. However as managers are more likely to be interested in what they can do to create and sustain their firm's success than in knowing about the types of routine they are dealing with, I have decided to include this discussion in the theoretical chapter.

Figure 13.1 is an elaboration of characteristic and linkage ambiguity from the managerial perspective. The figure is also based on a few assumptions. First, a distinction is drawn between the performers of the activities and

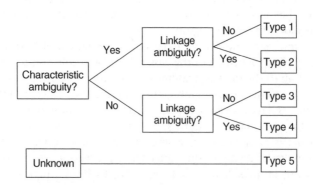

*Figure 13.1*   Combinations of characteristic and linkage ambiguity

those who are managing them. Obviously managers can themselves perform success-creating activities, but in the interest of clarity it is assumed here that managers are not involved in the routines in question. So the performers are the doers and not the managers of the routines, while the managers make decisions about routines, especially those which effect performance, but are not involved in the routines themselves. It is also assumed (and this is consistent with arguments in this book and in line with the resource-based argument) that the routines are valuable, that is, they have a positive impact on performance. The final assumption is that routines that display characteristic ambiguity to the performers also display characteristic ambiguity (or are unknown) to the managers, a not unreasonable assumption.

Reading from the left of the figure, routines are classified as either displaying characteristic ambiguity or not (the routine is not understood), or as being unknown to the managers. Then it is considered whether the routine is recognised by the managers as being valuable, that is, whether it displays linkage ambiguity. This generates four types of managerial causal ambiguity – the fifth results from the managers' lack of awareness of the routine.

*Type 1*   Type 1 routines are recognised by managers as being valuable but they do not fully comprehend them. The most appropriate response would be for managers to protect such a routine but not to intervene in it because they lack the necessary insight. However because they know it is valuable they can ensure that it is not inadvertently disturbed or even destroyed by an inappropriate action, such as cost cutting. Thus at best type 1 can be passively managed (left alone because they are causally ambiguous to the managers, see Chapter 9). The sustainability of the rents from these routines, *ceteris paribus*, should be enduring. The qualities of characteristic ambiguity that the routines possess should make it difficult for competitors to imitate them, and managers are alert to their significance. If the origins of the special qualities of the routines are partially understood, even if their performance is opaque to the managers the latter may at least be able to extend and preserve them by means of indirect socialisation processes.

*Type 2*   Type 2 routines are not understood by managers, nor do they recognise their positive impact on performance. These valuable routines are known about, but their value-generating significance is misunderstood and they are therefore vulnerable to inappropriate changes. They could be outsourced, 'improved' or even eliminated. Thus although characteristic ambiguity may protect them from imitation by competitors, they are at the mercy of misinformed management.

*Type 3*   Type 3 routines are well understood by managers and their value is recognised. These represent the bulk of organisational activities that are addressed in normal management discourse, particularly when managerial prescriptions are being discussed. Because these routines are understood and valued they can be actively managed (the managers can change them or leave them as they are, as deemed necessary). They can be further codified and taught to new employees, and they can be transferred to other parts of the organisation. They can also be made more efficient, and because their value-creating aspects are well understood they can be made even more effective, thus further enhancing their value. However the explicit and transparent nature of these valuable routines make them susceptible to imitation by competitors. Thus the rent stream accruing to them might be short-lived.

*Type 4*   Type 4 routines are understood but not valued. As with type 2 they are vulnerable to mismanagement, for example they might be eliminated by the actions of new managers entering the firm. Although the latter might understand the nature of the routines they do not recognise their significance. This could be due to their lack of insight into the idiosyncrasies of the firm and its customers. If a recently recruited executive is expected to bring about rapid and significant change, as in a turnaround situation, type 4 routines could be the first to be eliminated.

It may be the case that competitors are able both to understand and to recognise the value of these routines, and therefore try to replicate them or to hire the performers. Furthermore the firm's managers may not put up too much of a fight to hold on to these resources, given their lack of understanding about their true value.

*Type 5*   Managers are completely unaware of type 5 routines so cannot understand their value. Hence these routines are ignored. This can be due to executives lacking experience and insight into the operations they control, or being reluctant to learn about the organisation's processes. 'Management by walking about' would be one way of remedying this situation. Type 5 routines are completely unmanaged, endure by chance alone, and are vulnerable. Rents will accrue up to the point when the routines are eliminated by an uninformed management decision.

Until now only the managers' perspective has been taken into account, however it goes without saying that both characteristic ambiguity and linkage ambiguity can apply to the performers of routines as well as their managers, so in the following paragraphs some implications of causal ambiguity for the performers of valuable routines will be considered.

Performers may engage in routines that are characteristically ambiguous to them, that is, tacit or not fully understood. Here the interactions between employees may only be 'remembered in the doing'. In such cases there are severe constraints on the firm's ability to exploit or develop these resources.

The performers of valuable routines may also be unaware of the value of their contribution, that is, there is linkage ambiguity. One immediate consequence of this is that they reduce their chance of bargaining up their share of the value they create (Bowman and Ambrosini, 2000).

Clearly the situations described above do not cover all the combinations of linkage ambiguity between performers and managers, they are merely the most likely. For instance the performers could be aware of the value of their routines but the managers are not, and *vice versa*. This has a number implications, notably in terms of value capture. When it is difficult for performers to identify their contribution their bargaining power is reduced, whereas if both parties are aware of the routine's value informed negotiations can be expected. Moreover, if some routines have linkage ambiguity for the performers it may cause managers not to encourage or enhance valuable performance. If performers are unaware of the valuable aspects of their work it may be hard to get them to focus on these aspects and to perform them consistently. Managers may also find it difficult to persuade performers to pass on these valuable routines to others through training or indirect assimilation and socialisation.

### Routines and situational factors

At the end of Chapter 10 it was remarked that Alpha and Kappa differed markedly in terms of age, size, environment and tasks. It was also noted that Kappa's directors were still vital parts of the 'operating core' (to use Mintzberg's [1979] terminology), in contrast to Alpha, where the top managers were more separated from operational issues. This could explain some of the differences in their perceptions of ignorance and of explicit, tacit, and known but not understood routines (characteristic and linkage ambiguity). Hence it could be suggested that situational factors, or to use Mintzberg's (1979) term, 'contingency factors', influenced the types of routine that were perceived to be sources of success. Mintzberg identified the following factors: age, size, type of environment, task complexity and power relationships. In the following subsections some propositions are made about how these factors may influence explicit, tacit, ignored, and known but not understood routines as sources of organisational success.

### Age

- The younger the organisation the more likely it is that routines will be perceived as tacit and the less likely it is that they will be perceived as ignored, or known but not understood.

Over time managers have to think about how things are done, and as a result tacit routines may be made explicit. This may happen because new employees have to be trained. However training does not necessarily involve the transformation of tacit routines into explicit routines as it may take the form of an apprenticeship or any other method that involves observation and copying. Nonetheless if formal training does take place it is easier to teach routines that are articulated. Thus over time, as organisations mature, routines become systematised and codified, and therefore one can expect fewer tacit routines in older organisations than in younger ones. One could also argue that with age and systematisation, competing organisations tend to become more similar and their differences more subtle. This suggests that the part played by tacit routines in delivering advantage is crucial in mature organisations with few differential resources.

A counterargument to the proposition that age leads to systematisation is that over time routines are replicated in the firm but are only remembered in the doing, because those who prescribed them have long left or the reasons for the routine have been forgotten. Successful routines have become taken for granted.

It can also be argued that in a young organisation, an organisation with little history, managers are more likely to know and understand what is happening. It is only with time that routines are forgotten, or new routines are created without managers knowing about them or understanding their importance. In this respect it can be proposed that:

- If the managers who take part in a causal mapping workshop founded the organisation, the more likely it is that routines will be perceived as tacit and the less likely it is that they will be perceived as ignored, or known but not understood.

That is, if the current managers founded the company, the organisation is likely to be relatively young and the routines are likely to be tacitly known. Codification may not occur until new members are hired and other leave, the managers will whereupon have to explain their routines to others in order to reduce succession and growing problems for the organisation. The founding managers of a young company are likely to be very much in touch with what is happening. They have seen the routines develop and hence it is unlikely that there will be a great deal of ignorance.

*Size*

- The smaller the organisation the more likely it is that routines will be perceived as tacit and the less likely it is that they will be perceived as ignored, or known but not understood.

The reasoning behind this proposition is in some respects similar to the argument relating to age. Once the company grows larger the managers are unable to exert the same degree of direct control and have to start sharing their responsibilities. Hence they have to make some of their routines explicit so that others can take them over. Moreover as organisations grow larger they tend to become more formalised and hierarchical and the management role becomes more technocratic, so there is little room for tacit routines. Increase in organisational size is also often associated with increased organisational planning, and in order to plan their actions the members of the management team have to know what is happening. They are therefore motivated to explore routines explicitly. Similarly to what was said previously, if the organisation is small the managers are likely to know and understand what is happening. This may, however, be an intuitive understanding, and they are more likely to be directly involved in success-generating routines.

*Type of environment*

- The more dynamic the environment the more likely it is that routines will be perceived as tacit, ignored, or known but not understood.

Information that is gathered in a stable environment is usually more reliable than information gathered in an environment that is volatile and unpredictable. In a stable environment managers have time to collect information and check it. In an unstable environment managers may either have to deal with an absence of information, or with information that is unreliable because it has been poorly collected due to time pressures or is out of date because the environment is changing rapidly. This suggests that managers cannot rely on rational decision-making processes in dynamic environments and have to depend on their tacit routines. Judge and Miller (1991) argue that performance in dynamic environments is linked to fast decision making, based on experience. This link is not established in a stable environment, which suggests that almost immediate decisions and answers based on experience are necessary for good performance in unstable environments. It could also be added that in a stable environment managers have time to standardise their procedures and therefore it is likely that the proportion of explicit routines to tacit routines will be greater than in a dynamic environment.

As things change quickly in a dynamic environment, it is likely that there will be routines that managers do not know about or know about but do not understand because the environment is volatile and they have no time to reflect on their actions.

### Task complexity

- The more complex the internal environment the more likely it is that routines will be perceived as tacit, ignored, or known but not understood.

The complexity of the managers' task is likely to affect the extent to which they rely on tacit routines. The internal environment of an organisation is simple if its tasks can be broken down into easily understood actions. It is complex if the tasks cannot easily be broken down. If the tasks are simple they can be codified and therefore in a simple environment it is likely that tacit routines will not be heavily relied upon by the top management team. Conversely, complex tasks are likely to be difficult to describe fully and formalise, and therefore are likely to remain tacit. Complex tasks consist of various interrelated and difficult to identify elements, and this renders codification very difficult.

If the task is complex it is likely that some managers will not understand all the routines undertaken by the top management team, or even know that they are happening. This is the case not only because understanding a complex task is difficult but also because managers who carry out complex tasks will have little time to learn about and understand what is happening elsewhere in the organisation.

*Power relationships*

- The more externally controlled the organisation the less likely it is that routines will be perceived as tacit, ignored, or known but not understood.

If those in the top management team are controlled by external forces it is likely that the majority of their routines will be explicit, well known. This is the case because they are likely to be required to report on what they are doing, and in order to do so they have to express what they are doing. This formalises the routines and therefore they cannot remain tacit or unknown. External control also usually goes hand in hand with organisational planning and hence formalisation and codification.

If managers who take part in a causal mapping workshop relish power the routines revealed during the mapping session are likely to be perceived as tacit. In order to exert power managers have to be able to control what is happening in the company, and therefore they need to know and understand what it is that is happening. This leads to the formalisation of routines.

*Conclusion*

This subsection returns to findings obtained at Alpha, Kappa and Delta in order to examine whether they support the propositions presented above. Obviously, in order to explore these ideas fully, multiple studies would be necessary, so the findings merely provide an indication that examining the links between situational factors, types of routine and types of organisation could be an interesting avenue for empirical research.

Mintzberg (1983) describes how some organisational structures are frequently associated with certain situational factors. Briefly, he explains that a simple structure is typically young, small, operates in a dynamic environment, has simple tasks and external control is weak. An operating ad hocracy is usually young, small, operates in a dynamic environment, has complex tasks, external control is weak and the exercise of power in relationships is weak. Finally, a machine bureaucracy and a divisionalised organisation are similar: they are typically old, large, operate in a stable environment, have simple tasks, external control is strong and the exercise of power in relationships is strong.

The differing combinations of contingency factors operating in Mintzberg's configurations suggest a stronger or weaker tendency for the existence of tacit routines. Contingency factors that indicate the likely presence of tacit routines (or any other categories) may not match the propositions (for instance a dynamic environment suggests the presence of tacit routines whereas a simple task suggests the contrary, yet both factors apply to the simple structure), but if the factors could be weighted there might be some avenues for research and some interesting results could be produced. We shall look now at the three main case study firms.

Alpha was an old and large organisation. It operated in a stable environment and its tasks were relatively simple (selling and managing pensions). External control (government regulations) was strong, as was the exercise of power by some directors. Kappa was young and small, operated in a dynamic environment and its tasks were complex (management consultancy services). There was little external control. Delta was young and large, operated in a stable environment and its tasks were now relatively simple (selling and servicing one item of software) – task complexity had probably ended 8–10 years previously when the software was designed. There was strong control by the parent company and the CEO relished the exercise of power. According to Mintzberg's configurations, Alpha was a machine bureaucracy, Kappa an operating ad hocracy and Delta a divisionalised form.

With the caveats that the perception of tacitness is personal and different people use different categories, the findings of the studies (Chapters 7, 10 and 11) show that little was ignored at Kappa, the operating ad hocracy, where the partners had founded the organisation and were still part of the operating core, and a lot of routines were tacit or not known across the organisation because they had never been communicated. At Alpha, where most directors were not involved in the operating core and where external control and the exercise of power by the CEO were strong, there was little tacitness but a fair number of routines were not well understood. At Delta, where the parent company exerted strong control and the CEO was powerful, ignorance was a real issue and a number of factors were tacit. None of these findings contradict the propositions. They are incomplete, but some interesting implications have been drawn, a further avenue for research has been exposed and a better understanding of routines has been developed.

### Towards a model of routines as a source of organisational success

This subsection highlights some of the contributions made by the research. It concentrates on the part played by routines in firms' success as, to quote Ireland *et al.*, (2001, p. 53), 'the primary interest of strategy

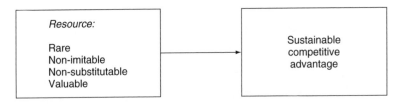

*Figure 13.2*   Basic argument of the resource-based view

management researchers is to explain differential firm performance'. The framework that follows is in some respects analogous to 'diagramming' my argument.

When drawing the framework a few restrictions were made: it is limited to organisations that operate in a competitive market, it only deals with routines that are perceived to have a positive effect on performance, and explicit routines (ones that can be easily imitated) are not considered. The process of developing the framework is traced below.

Figure 13.2 summarises the basic argument of the resource-based view.

One example of such a resource is tacit knowledge, so the model can be simplified to that depicted in Figure 13.3.

The present research has shown that in an organisational context, tacit knowledge is best understood as tacit routines, and it has been argued that managers' accounts of their firm's success is an acceptable proxy for sustainable competitive advantage as there is no widely accepted measure of SCA. The model now becomes that shown in Figure 13.4.

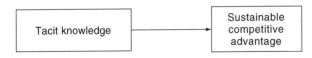

*Figure 13.3*   Tacit knowledge is rare, non-imitable, non-substitutable and valuable

*Figure 13.4*   The operationalisation of tacit knowledge as a source of sustainable competitive advantage

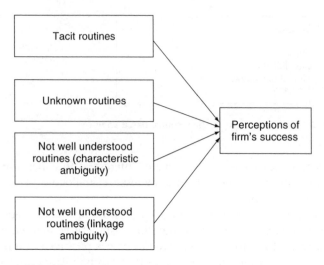

*Figure 13.5*    Valuable routine

It has been empirically shown that tacit routines are perceived by managers to be a component of their firm's success, thus confirming the conceptual argument. However other valuable routines are also revealed (Figure 13.5).

The framework in Figure 13.5 has direct managerial implications and hence it can be further developed (Figure 13.6).

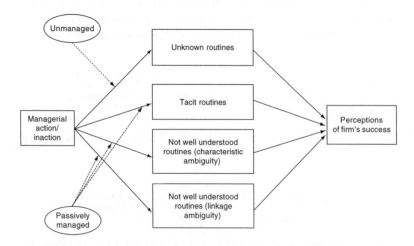

*Figure 13.6*    Managerial action and valuable routine

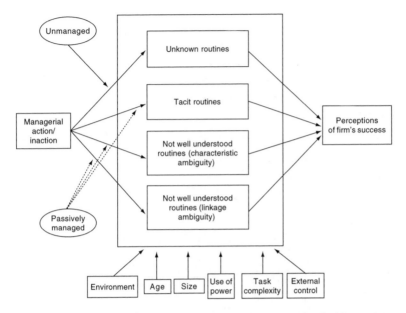

*Figure 13.7* The external environment, managerial action and valuable routine

When discussing the situations in which tacit, ignored or not well understood routines occur, it was suggested that size, age, use of power, external control, the environment and task complexity have an impact (Figure 13.7).

Finally, the model can be enriched by adding elements such as the vulnerability of firms' success that we discussed earlier (Figure 13.8).

## Final comments

The proposition that tacit, not well understood or ignored routines – which may be passively managed or entirely unmanaged – might play a crucial part in organisational success leads us to question even the most rational approaches to strategic management. It is an extremely arduous if not impossible task to plan and analyse something that one does not understand very well. The resource-based view of the firm concentrates on what is happening inside the firm (Barney, 1995) and on what is unique to each organisation. If routines are a source of advantage, what causes success in an organisation is idiosyncratic to

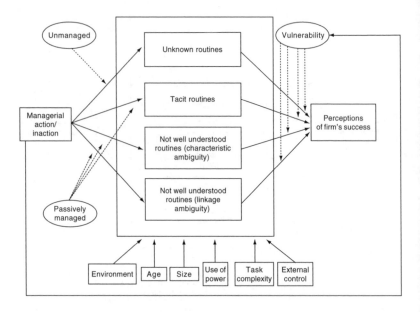

*Figure 13.8*   A model of organisational routines as a source of organisational success

that organisation, that is, one cannot copy a 'recipe' (Spender, 1989) from one firm to another. Therefore 'generic strategies' (Porter, 1980) are the equivalent of tangible resources. They are available to any organisation, and therefore knowledge of them cannot lead to advantage. Idiosyncrasy and the limitations of generic strategies mean that, for instance, cost cutting as a tactic will not have long-term benefits. Cost cutting is easy to understand, relatively easy to implement, lends itself to measurement and control and as such is a tactic that managers tend to employ. Cost cutting does enable managers to avoid uncertainty and ambiguity, however it is a well trodden 'recipe'. Everybody knows how to do it and hence it can be executed by all, its supposed benefits being reaped by most firms. In other words cost cutting will only help an organisation to remain competitive, it will not enable it to move ahead of its competitors. This has direct managerial implications, and these will be addressed in the next chapter.

# 14
## Managerial Implications

This chapter addresses the more practical implications of the research. Many of these are intertwined with the theoretical implications discussed previously and a few were attended to when concluding the chapters relating to Alpha, Kappa and Delta. The aim here is not to revisit these but to draw some more general conclusions.

### The managerial relevance of mapping organisational success

#### Eliciting valuable routines

Before going any further it should be acknowledged that doubts could be raised about the value of identifying tacit routines. If tacit routines are a component of a firm's success it is because they cannot be replicated, transferred from firm to firm. If they are made explicit they become easier to imitate by other firms, and consequently they can no longer be a source of sustainable competitive advantage for the original firm. To a certain extent this argument is fair. However it is certainly more compelling theoretically than empirically. As the maps have shown, the success of an organisation is based on a complex pattern of interlinked, context-specific activities, and a single specific element cannot be isolated as the sole source of success (Dierickx and Cool, 1989). This means that 'even if we could point to the critical links and more or less reproduce them, we still could not reproduce all the relationships or the external environment in which they operate' (Reichheld, 1996, p. 60). In other words, even if one organisation could see the maps of its competitors it is highly unlikely that it would be able to reproduce the systems that cause success. Moreover 'because routines are formed from the very particular historical and current combination of organisational features (people, structures, technologies etc.), they are impossible to replicate or "buy-in"' (Tranfield and Smith, 1998, p. 119). In short, because routines are context-dependent 'the effectiveness of a routine is not measured by what is achieved in principle but by what is achieved in practice; this generally means that the routines might be declared effective in some specific contexts, but perhaps not in others' (Cohen *et al.*, 1996, p. 662).

Another issue that needs to be addressed is why bother looking at the present (and therefore at *past* routines) when it could be argued that organisations should concentrate on the future. Several arguments have been raised in favour of doing so. For example Eden and Ackermann (1998, p. 108) explain that the 'basic knowledge and awareness of distinctive competencies must start with an appreciation of what strengths an organisation has and how its current success originated, before any attempt can be made to consider the future'. Brown and Eisenhard (1998) take a similar view and argue that if a business is to evolve faster and more effectively than its competitors it is important to build on its strengths, to draw on the past. By doing so it can avoid duplicating what is happening elsewhere in the firm, little needs to be invented from scratch. Brown and Eisenhard suggest that by knowing the present, managers can blend it with something new. The present can be exploited and refreshed while the new is being created.

So for the organisation whose managers are able to elicit some of its successful routines the payoff can be important. The managers can begin to better understand how these routines are connected, discuss their value, and decide what should be promoted and developed and what should be modified or discarded. Tacit routines is the first step towards exploiting these routines and leveraging what they are good. Managers can focus on the efficiency or effectiveness of the routines and consider whether they should be applied throughout the organisation. They can also adopt what March (1991) calls an 'exploitative' learning approach, that is, learning how to improve what they already do. Obviously the routines will also need to be protected. In short, managers can start work on nurturing their most important assets for the future.

In the previous chapter (see the section on valuable routines), the consequences of ignorance, tacitness and causal ambiguity were dealt with in terms of what managers can do, how sustainable their success is and who is most likely to capture value in the organisation. This can be regarded as a managerial benefit as the role of managers may be severely limited if they do not attempt to gain a better understanding of how success is generated in their organisation.

## Practical benefits

In the chapters relating to Alpha, Kappa and Delta the practical consequences of the routines revealed by the participants in the mapping sessions were considered. These were conclusions of what the mapping could tell each organisation, and notably which activities might need protection or were very vulnerable because they were not understood or were ignored by some senior managers. At this point it will be interesting to note some of the participants' comments about the benefits of causally mapping organisational success. We shall concentrate on aspects they specifically stressed, that surprised them or that they found most beneficial.

For the Alpha participants what was most striking was how dependent the organisation was on the CEO (and therefore how crucial the question of succession was), and how little they actually understood or knew what was happening in their organisation. In particular they had never recognised the true value of their young employees, who did not mind working overtime for no extra pay as they enjoyed working together and socialising in London. Relocating and employing people who only wanted to work eight hours a day for five days a week could reduce their costs but it might also damage their effectiveness in delivering a responsive service.

Delta's commercial director wrote to tell me that the participants had found the session very useful and thought provoking. As at Alpha, the mapping had revealed a number of success factors that had not been well known or discussed in the company and the commercial director considered that they needed to think about how discussion of these factors could be encouraged and built upon. He commented on the value of learning (a) that different people had different perceptions of the causes of Delta's success, and (b) that colleagues who had contributed to Delta's sales success had strong opinions about their contribution. The session had also raised a number of questions about the sort of company that Delta was. The map had shown that in reality it was virtually a one-product company (developing, selling and servicing the software) and not what it should be – a solutions company, selling a range of products and services to the sector in which it had particular business and technical expertise.

The participants at Kappa were very excited about the session because it had genuinely helped them to understand what their success was based on. They thought that the session had helped to 'crystallise what was in their heads' and to define what they were about. Until then they had always struggled with the issue. The map had broadened what they had traditionally thought of as their areas of business and made them think about the implications of this for their knowledge requirements. Thanks to the session they had been able to draw a picture of the business, and as a result they had redefined what they were offering to their customers and what the company was about. Until the session they had seen themselves as offering five products: brand development, strategy and policy development, change management, customer service and network performance improvement. Now they were about 'customer R&D' – the application of knowledge, ideas and tools to help their customers' development – and saw themselves as working with, not for, their clients. It is worth adding that because they found the causal mapping session and the use of examples and storytelling beneficial they had begun to use it in other parts of the business with various groups of employees in order to gain an even better grasp of what made the company successful.

This reinforces the proposition that the real benefit of uncovering valuable routines is not to find out what is tacit and what is not, but to give managers a better understanding of how their organisation works, to discover what they need to manage in order for the organisation to sustain its success. What matters to managers is not the nature of the constructs they have revealed but what generates success in their organisation, why this is so and how it can be sustained and developed.

## The vulnerability of organisational success and the role of managers

The case studies revealed that among the activities that are a source of organisational success, many of them – because they are tacit, not well understood (in short displaying characteristic and linkage ambiguity) or ignored – are not actively managed but are only passively managed or even unmanaged. This certainly raises questions about the fragility of firms' success and the role of managers in sustaining advantage.

If ways of operating that are unknown or not well known play a crucial role and are the main source of difference between organisations – rather than, say, tangible resources – this means that what gives organisations their edge lies at the margin of managerial understanding. A major implication of this is that success based on those routines is vulnerable. There are several reasons why this is so.

The first reason lies in the nature of ignored and causally ambiguous activities. Because managers are not precisely aware of which routines are sources of positive advantage and how they are performed, they might inadvertently change something that is crucial, for example through delayering or business process re-engineering. Moreover 'an organisation cannot improve that which it does not understand' (Teece *et al.*, 1997, p. 525), so recognising the existence of the phenomenon is essential if managers are to make beneficial decisions. These issues were referred to in Chapter 13 when discussing the theoretical implications of valuable routines.

Organisational success can also be made vulnerable by the attitude of managers towards routines: as has been shown, they may not know that some routines matter or they may not care about them. Top managers may pay scant attention to the detail of what is happening in the organisation. Generally speaking they are encouraged and expected to address the 'big picture', the strategic agenda of the organisation; they are not encouraged or expected to engage in the small details. However in order to discover which routines affect organisational performance the organisation must be studied in detail, including how its various members interact and what they are doing precisely. Senior managers are likely to be well aware of the policies that are being espoused, but not of the *how*, other than a peripheral awareness of routines in a particular subset of the organisation, based on their past functional experience. This can be related to the situational factors mentioned in Chapter 13, and it can be conjectured that it is most likely to be the case in large organisations, where the top managers are less likely to be part of the operating core and therefore are not involved in day-to-day operations. They view the precise ways of doing things as a concern for the shop floor. Knowledge of the detailed running of the operations is usually not seen as being of strategic value and therefore routines that contribute to superior performance are overlooked. Hence they are not protected and nurtured and as a consequence may be inadvertently annihilated.

The above arguments suggest that the role of managers and strategists, and their vocabulary, may have to change. Perhaps 'strategy' should be understood as 'recognising organisational routines' and 'managing' should involve protecting, nurturing and leveraging rather than controlling, directing, monitoring and planning. That is, 'The senior manager's task [should] change . . . from direction and control to development and support' (Bartlett and Ghoshal, 1997, p. 99). Managers must start to understand that details matter, that routines that create value have to be nurtured and possibly transferred to other parts of the organisation where they could be of value.

## Leveraging routines

As already explained, tacit, ignored, and known but not understood routines can be sources of difference between organisations and hence sources of competitive advantage, but ignorance of their existence renders them vulnerable. Indeed if managers are unaware of these routines they may inadvertently change them or even destroy them, for instance during the course of downsizing. This is why managers must try to identify their organisation's valuable routines, even if it is difficult to do so.

When valuable ways of operating are identified managers can not only protect them from change but also investigate their interconnections, discuss their value, and decide what they should promote and develop or modify or discard. Success-generating tacit activities mark the starting point of a process of exploiting them, leveraging what the firm is good at. This can be important when, for instance, organisations are envisaging merging or forming an alliance, because they need to know what causes their success, what they are really good at, in order to have solid ground upon which to base their decisions. Finally, tacit, passively managed and unmanaged routines in different parts of the organisation or for different markets can reveal that success is not caused by the same factors across the organisation. This can indicate where routines could be transferred across the organisation for success and lead to a better-informed restructuring of activities.

Successful routines will be worth leveraging if they can bring further advantage to the organisation by being deployed in a new way, for instance in another product domain. They may also be worth leveraging if they can be extended at low cost, for example without damaging the effectiveness of their present deployments or if they are currently underutilised.

Leveraging tacit and not well understood routines is likely to be very difficult as they are not codified. They could be leveraged by moving the performers of the routines to other subunits of the organisation. However this will mean that the performers' original unit will be deprived, and it may be the case that the transferred routine will not have the required complementary resources in its new context for it to be truly effective.

The most challenging routines to develop will be tacit or not well understood routines that are firm-specific and complex. It will be difficult to set out an explicit action plan to develop them, so rather than moving the people who perform the routines the transfer is likely to involve a process of experimentation. This may be funded and guided by the centre, but may equally emerge from initiatives undertaken spontaneously at many levels of the structure. For this haphazard and ad hoc development process to be stimulated, development by the leadership of a culture that encourages such behaviour is required.

## Implications for managerial education and strategy consulting

Two managerial implications that have arisen from the case studies are that managers must recognise the importance of organisational routines, and that they need to take more interest in the small details of how their organisation operates. The findings also question the stress put on managers as 'planners', as it is difficult to plan something that is poorly understood or whose effects are unknown. The examination of routines that are unmanaged or passively managed is a research agenda that goes in the direction advocated by Mosakowski (1998, p. 1179), who wrote that 'strategic management scholars should not contribute to the myth of complete managerial control'.

Very often management courses focus on theory rather than practice, teaching abstract knowledge rather than know-how as on the whole Western societies tend to believe that abstract knowledge is superior to practice (Nonaka and Takeuchi, 1995). Theories provide an understanding of organisations and how they operate and do not usually deal with the immediate problems that managers are facing, but this does not mean that they are not important to managerial practice as they can provide useful insights to guide decision making. However without informed practical research, actions may be taken on the basis of anecdotes, or taken out of context. Furthermore the emphasis on theory might cause managers or future managers to accord little value to practical details, to specific organisational operations. Hence they are likely to disregard them rather than to consider them as potential sources of competitive advantage. In other words,

> in a society that attaches particular value to 'abstract knowledge', the details of practice have come to be seen as nonessential, unimportant, and easily developed once the relevant abstractions have been grasped. Thus education, training, and technology design generally focus on abstract representations to the detriment, if not exclusion of actual practice. (Brown and Dugruid, 1991, p. 40)

These two points suggest that passively managed and unmanaged routines not only have managerial implications, but also have implications for management education. As Sparrow (1998, pp. 3, 10) remarks, 'manage-ment education's emphasis on the "sciences" manifests a drive for certainty and non-recognition of the value of ambiguity', despite the fact that 'the notion of decision processes in organisations being driven by rationality is recognised to be unrealistic'. If management courses empha-sise the theoretical side of management and management is taught as a generic activity, this could affect organisations' ability to create and sustain competitive advantage, as according to the resource-based view a generic activity cannot be a source of differential value. If all managers manage in a similar way because of their management education, this could partly explain why routines that are left unmanaged or are passively managed can be a source of advantage: activities that are not managed are possible sources of success because they are less likely to be performed similarly across organisations. This does not necessarily imply that either educators or managers are at fault. Each group evolves in a different sphere of thought (Dougherty, 1992), may have a different agenda or does not have the same priorities.

Causal mapping of how success is generated in an organisation high-lights the interconnectedness of organisational routines and the com-plexity of the process of success-generation. But as Baets (1998, p. 94) asserts, 'managers do not feel comfortable with uncertainties and further-more we are taught we cannot manage what we cannot observe and/or make explicit. Only in these terms making explicit often means describ-ing it in linear, non-dynamic systems.' This is also a reason why managers may not recognise the importance of unmanaged or passively managed routines. They are not comfortable with what they do not understand and cannot easily control, which is not helped by the fact that the 'soft' aspects of management, such as the use of intuition, are not as respected as the hard side of management (control, analysis, command and so on).

This implication for managers and managerial education is also applicable to some management consultants. The consultants' role is characteristically about guiding and facilitating the strategic process, providing managers with direction and rigour in their decision making. In order to do so they often use theoretical frameworks and tools, and one of their tasks is to ensure that these theory-driven frameworks are understood in the context of the daily reality of the business to which they are applied. The question is whether these help managers to explore difficult issues that they may not want to deal with, such as ignorance. Moreover, strategy advisers will find it difficult to make prescriptions if they employ an analytic method that fails to elicit tacit, ignored and not well understood routines.

# 15
## Conclusion

Before summarising this book it is necessary to mention some limitations of the research that have not been fully discussed so far.

### Limitations

First, it is not claimed here that one has established an exclusive link between tacit routines – or any other routines – and competitive advantage, or that any definitive conclusions can be drawn from single case studies. Only new and more developed insights into organisations have been offered. There is no single factor that causes success on its own, and the types of routine in the study will be just some of many. Despite employing the expression 'mapping organisational success', it is obvious that only a fraction of the causes of success in organisations can practically be mapped. Constraint on time is one of the main reasons for this, not to mention the impossibility of the task due to the intricacy, size and ever-changing nature of organisations. Even if it were possible, mapping a full organisation would take weeks. Another reason is that the maps were constructed by particular groups of managers and only their perceptions of success were recorded. Ideally a large proportion of the staff in the organisations concerned should have taken part. Moreover, not only was the number of participants limited, but what these participants could recall or were willing to express was also limited.

It should also be added that the goal of the causal mapping was to reveal routines that were responsible for current success so that managers would be able to nurture them. However what was working then cannot be guaranteed to be appropriate in the future.

Another limitation, as mentioned at the start of the book, was that the study concentrated exclusively on routines that were perceived to cause success. To obtain a more complete picture it would be necessary to look at routines that lead to failure. Therefore a mirror opposite of the current study would be an appropriate research project in the future.

Finally, I would like to quote Jenkins (1998, p. 243), who argues that 'it is unacceptable in today's lean times for managers to spend up to nine hours with a researcher unless there are clear direct benefits from this use of time' and 'the most rigorous methodology is meaningless if you cannot get managers to take part in the research'.

## Summary

Summarising a book is undoubtedly about choosing and, it is to be hoped, striking the right balance between repeating too much or saying too little. The next few paragraphs will therefore concentrate on the skeleton of the book.

What motivated the research was an obvious gap in the strategic management literature, and in particular that on the resource-based view of the firm. It has been widely acknowledged that tacit knowledge is a crucial source of competitive advantage, however the literature on the subject has remained mainly conceptual and no substantial empirical work has been conducted. The aim of the research was to help fill this gap.

This book began by reviewing the tacit knowledge literature and explaining that the main reasons why tacit knowledge is so crucial to organisational success are its immobility and inimitability. Then tacit knowledge was defined in such a way that it became amenable to operationalisation. This was done by showing that organisational tacit knowledge could be understood as tacit routines. Then a method of empirically charting tacit routines in organisations was introduced, and it was shown that causal mapping is a simple but powerful technique to elicit such routines. One of the most notable aspects of the technique is that it facilitates the identification of organisational idiosyncrasies. By continually asking the same questions, such as 'What do you do that causes success?', 'What causes that?', participants are encouraged to reflect on what they are doing, to uncover what they would not normally talk about. The process is helped further by encouraging the participants to give examples and tell stories.

Causal mapping reflects the participants' organisational reality much better than an imposed structure stemming from a value chain or an organisational chart. It clearly reveals and acknowledges that an organisation is a complex entity. The mapping process gives the participants and the researcher a greater understanding of how the firm works, and where some of its unknown or not understood sources of success lie.

One of the main findings of the research is that there are many types of routine that lead to organisational success, and that the basic distinction between tacit and explicit is not advanced enough to allow a detailed description of all the causes of success. In particular the empirical research has revealed that it is not only tacit routines that can be perceived as a component of firms' positive performance, but routines that are not understood can also be as crucial. The features of these and how they work are not understood, or their link with performance is unknown. Another conclusion is that some vital routines are unknown to the managers of the organisation. This implies that some sources of success are unmanaged, they are left to continue as they are because managers do not know of their existence.

The causal mapping process may be perceived by managers as not 'strategic'. Very often strategy is associated with prescription, with direction and control and with tangible variables, the mapping process does not provide a recipe or solution, it does not tell managers what to do. It is about understanding a business, not about 'strategy', and hence maybe disconcerting, if not frustrating, for certain participants. In spite of this the process raises important issues as far as the role of managers and strategic management are concerned. It can reveal that managers do not necessarily understand the processes behind their organisation's performance. If, as found, many ways of doing things in organisations are tacit, not well understood or ignored, the causes of advantage in organisations can become vulnerable: if senior managers do not know why the organisation is succeeding they can very easily destroy these sources of advantage, for instance through inappropriate cost-cutting measures. If routines are not recognised as important, little or no effort will be made to protect or develop them, and hence they are in danger of being neglected or eradicated.

# Appendix 1: Interview Schedule for Alpha

## 1 Semistructured interview

### Introduction (5 minutes)

This interview is being carried out as preparatory work for the strategy workshop to be held in Cranfield on 3 February.

The main goal of the interview is to find out what you believe are the main reasons for Alpha's success.

The interview is informal and you must feel free to tell me anything that comes to mind, even if it might be irrelevant. Think of the interview as a bit like a brainstorming session. If you think of, let's say, a cat, then say it as this may trigger some interesting thoughts.

I would like to tape the interview if that is alright with you, but everything you say will be kept confidential. While we might use some parts of the interview in the group session to be held in Cranfield, your name will not be attached to it. For instance if you tell me that Alpha is performing very well because its offices are in London, we may use this statement for the group discussion, but nobody will know that this was your idea.

Before going to the core of the subject I would like to ask you a couple of facts:

- How long have you been working for Alpha?
- What was (or were) your previous function(s) at Alpha?

### Interview (10 minutes per question)

1. I would like you to talk about why you think Alpha is a successful organisation. I am interested in the fundamental reasons for this success. I want you to try to get to heart of the matter. For instance if you think that Alpha is successful because of its low cost, then try to think of reasons why this is so. It is like peeling an onion, removing the layers one by one to reach the core. *Probe*: success = performance, competitive advantage or edge, investment returns, market share customer satisfaction, unit cost per member? Metaphors Style Culture.
2. What is it that makes Alpha so special/unique (what activities/processes are unique)? *Probe*: culture, people, work for charity, location.
3. Could you please describe one situation, something that happened that brought success to the organisation [or, could you reflect on one particular incident that led to a positive outcome for Alpha/just describe a particular circumstance or set of events that led to great performance – performance meaning whatever the interviewee wants it to mean]. *Probe*: activity, process, team of people, specific individual, customer, luck.

4. Could you narrate what happened one time when Alpha was rather unsuccessful? *Probe*: activity, process, team of people, specific individual, customer, luck.
5. Are there any stories that are always told to newcomers to the organisation? *Probe*: example, the IBM story–young recruit refused to let the CEO of IBM enter one of the organisation's factories because he was not wearing the right badge.

### Conclusion (5 minutes)

Thanks a lot for your help. Do you want to add anything to what you have said? If you think of anything else please feel free to contact me. See you on 3 February.

## 2  Self-Q

Introduction and conclusion as per interview. As I have mentioned, this interview is about the factors that contribute to Alpha's success. You are the expert on your view of Alpha. What I would like you to do is to ask yourself questions about Alpha's performance, but please do not try to answer these questions. While you're asking yourself the questions I may scribble down a few words. [I place on the interview table a piece of paper with 'Factors that contribute to Alpha's success' written at the top.]

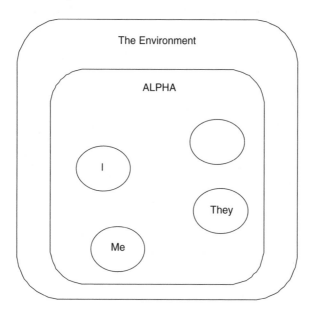

You may be surprised that I have asked you to ask yourself questions, and perhaps you're a bit puzzled, but in fact we ask questions ourselves every day, although most of the time we are simply not aware of it. For instance when you get up you may ask yourself 'Do I want breakfast?' 'Am I late?' 'What am I going to wear?'

Basically I just want you to ask yourself questions about Alpha and its performance. Ask any questions, simple or complicated, it does not matter as you do not have to give any answers! [If the interviewee stalls I present the following diagram to prompt him or her to ask questions.]

This circle represents Alpha. The larger circle represents the larger context in which you consider Alpha. This represents you (I), you looking at yourself (me) and others (they). This is whatever you want, a team, a department, a network and so on.

For instance you could ask questions about your role in Alpha (questions from I to me), your contacts with others (questions from I to they), what people might think about you and your role in the success of Alpha (questions from they to me). You could also ask questions about Alpha and its environment, its environment and you and so on.

# Appendix 2: Factors Perceived to Contribute to Alpha's Success

- Niche market.
- Massive market.
- Expanding market.
- Charity market.
- No earnings go to third parties.
- CEO is singled minded.
- CEO is always a step ahead.
- CEO anticipates events.
- CEO would not have done well without the market situation and if Alpha had to give away earnings.
- CEO left alone by trustees.
- CEO's drive.
- CEO's vision.
- Charismatic CEO.
- High-profile CEO.
- CEO well thought of in the external world.
- CEO a champion.
- CEO's ideas.
- CEO forces things through.
- CEO's longevity.
- CEO leads by example: he works hard so we do too.
- We accept everybody (small and big employers).
- People trained beyond their job needs.
- Alpha believes it has a responsibility for its employees' future.
- Complaints dealt with by CEO.
- Alpha is seen as practising what it preaches.
- Views of staff are taken on board.
- Everybody involved in business plan.
- Employee involvement in project – implement their decisions without reporting to management.
- Integrity of people.
- Commitment of people.
- People work long hours.
- Dedication of staff.
- Staff are performance geared.
- Values.
- People understand what they do.
- Recession had no impact.
- Integration of new people not too difficult.
- Alpha is synonymous with CEO.
- EMT's (top management team) networking.
- Inflation-proofing requirement.
- The members are customers – not employers.

- Combination of board of trustees and CEO.
- Alpha takes care of the situation of people retiring or leaving early.
- Safety/security in brand.
- Total service package.
- Clear focus: Alpha offers pensions.
- People's/trustees' recommendations.
- Little money spent on advertising.
- Wide range of schemes offered.
- People trust Alpha.
- Luck.
- Role of trustees and EMT well defined.
- We are dealing with people's needs, not wants – we do not sell products to people if they do not need them.
- Alpha is honest – tells the truth.
- Investment returns.
- High-profile clients attract others.
- Success built on success.
- Trustees good at networking for Alpha.
- Trustee involvement (not too much, but still there).
- Trustees provide bedrock of security for clients.
- Leading provider in the field.
- Growth is good.
- EMT consists of fiercely independent people.
- Big new award scheme.
- We offer the right type of service.
- We have same ethos as our clients.
- We deliver.
- We are successful because we want to be.
- Continuity in EMT.
- Good to appear democratic.
- Good advisers.
- The EMT people have a different view of how Alpha should develop.
- Good balance between trustees/CEO and EMT staff.
- Clean image.
- Good name.
- Alpha has empathy with the values of its market.
- We understand charities better than our competitors do.
- Quality of service.
- Being in the right place at the right time.
- Individual contacts.
- Business planning process.
- We do not try to do more of the same.
- Planning for the future.
- Customer focus.
- Reasonable control of costs.
- Scope for cutting costs.

# Appendix 3: Maps Generated During Alpha's Causal Mapping Session

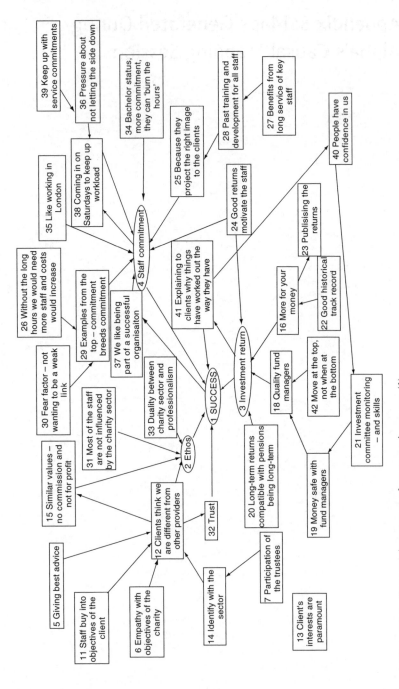

*Figure A3.1* Directors' accounts of company's success (1)

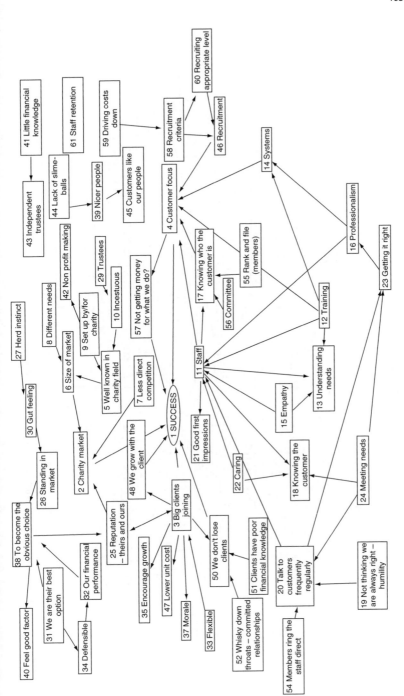

*Figure A3.2* Directors' accounts of company's success (2)

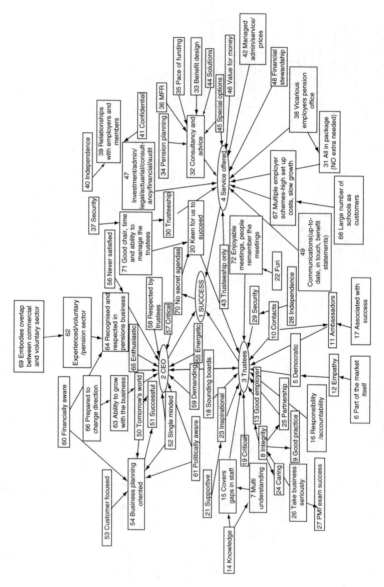

*Figure A3.3*　Directors' accounts of company's success (3)

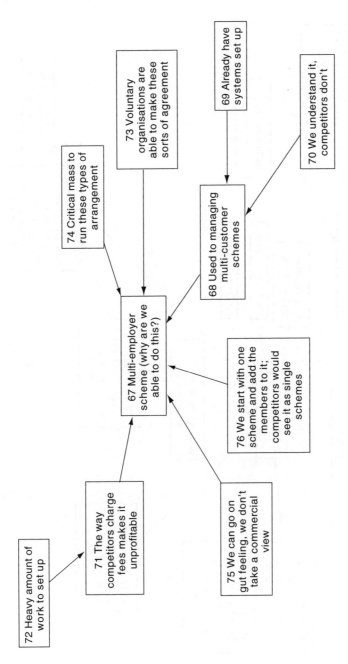

*Figure A3.4* Multi

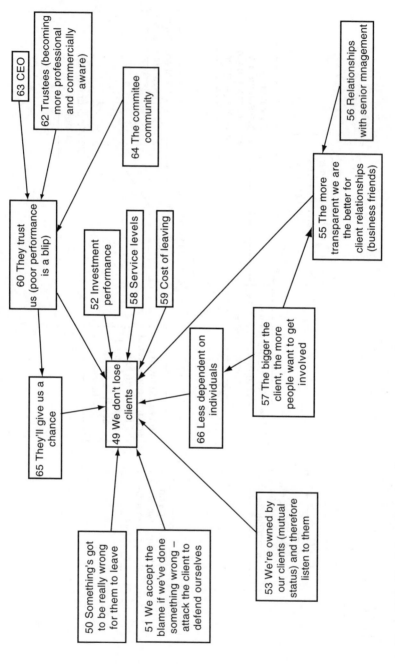

*Figure A3.5*  Don't lose clients map!

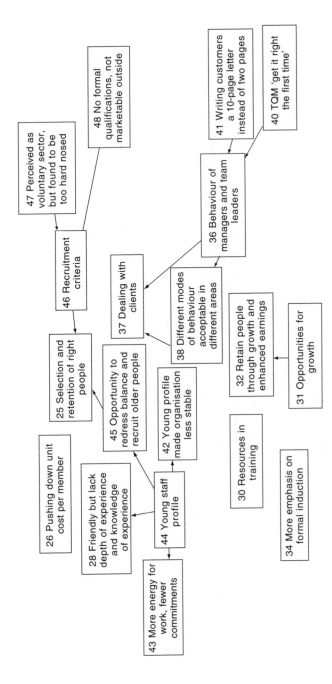

*Figure A3.6* Recruitment and selection map

168

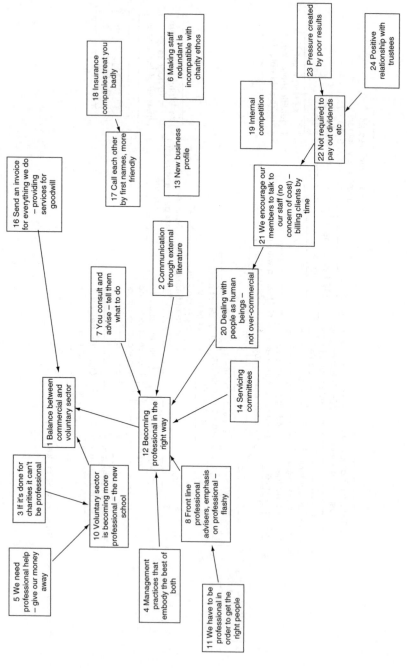

*Figure A3.7*  Balance map

# Appendix 4: Maps Generated During Kappa's Causal Mapping Session

170

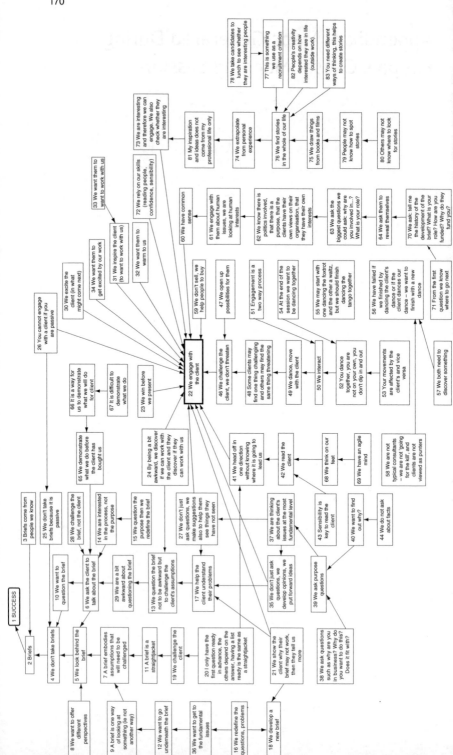

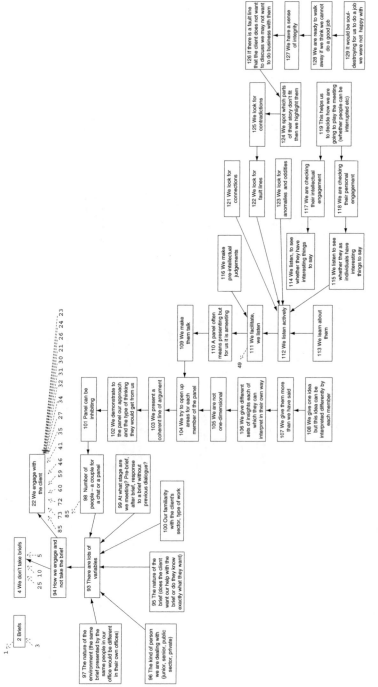

171

*Figure A4.2* Engagements with clients and dealing with a panel

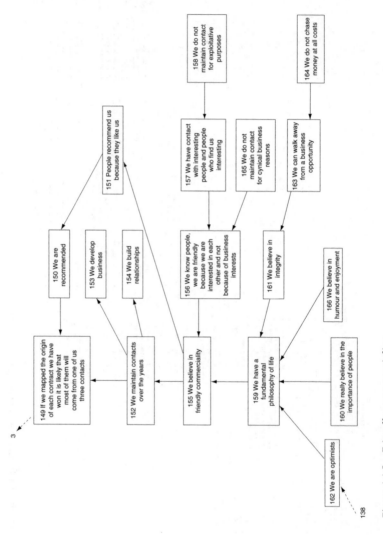

*Figure A4.3*  Friendly commerciality

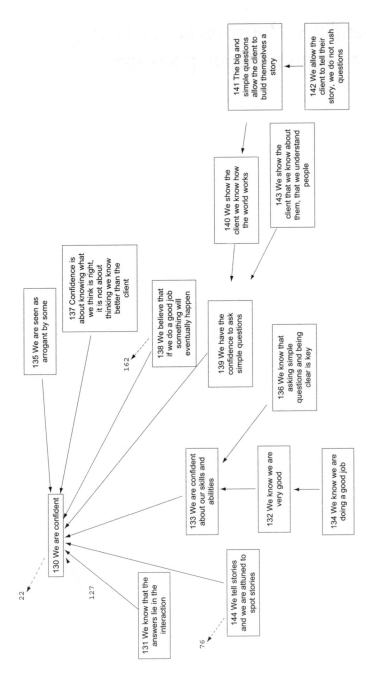

*Figure A4.4* Confidence

# Appendix 5: Maps Generated During Delta's Causal Mapping Session

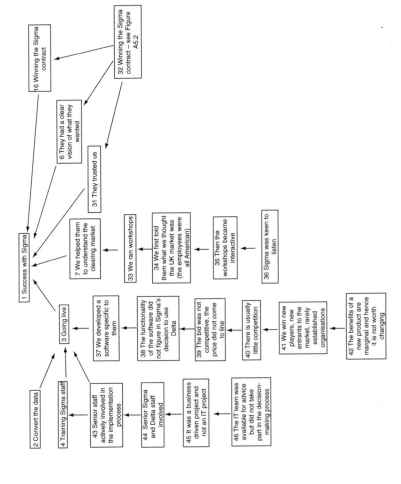

*Figure A5.1* Going live with Sigma

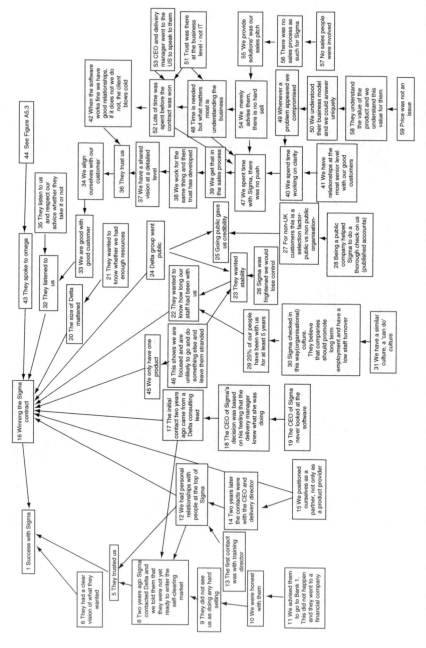

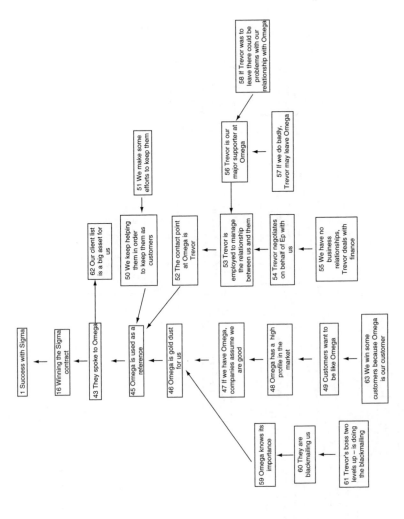

*Figure A5.3*  Omega

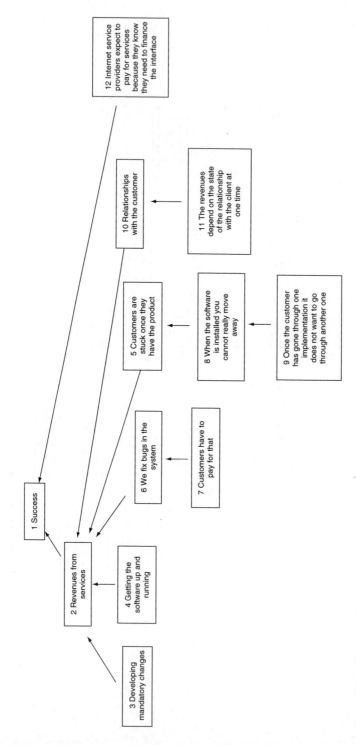

*Figure A5.4* Revenues from services

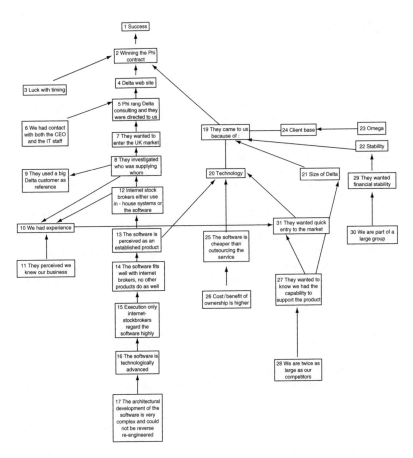

*Figure A5.5*  Phi

# References

Ackermann, F. (1996) 'Participants' perceptions on the role of facilitators using group decision support systems', *Group Decision and Negotiation*, vol. 5, pp. 93–112.

Adler, P. S. and A. Shenbar (1990) 'Adapting your technological base: the organisational challenge', *Sloan Management Review*, Fall, pp. 25–37.

Agarwal, R. and M. R. Tanniru (1990) 'Knowledge acquisition using structured interviewing: an empirical investigation', *Journal of Management and Information Systems*, vol. 7, no. 1, pp. 123–40.

Agnew, N. M., K. M. Ford and P. J. Hayes (1994) 'Expertise in context: personally constructed, socially selected, and reality relevant?', *International Journal of Expert Systems*, vol. 7, no. 1, pp. 65–88.

Alchian, A. A. and H. Demsetz (1972) 'Production, information costs, and economic organization', *The American Economic Review*, December, pp. 777–95.

Ambrosini, V. (1996) 'Tacit knowledge?', paper presented at the Third IFSAM World Conference, Paris, Proceedings, p. 58.

Ambrosini, V. (2002a) 'Bridging the worlds of academia and business: understanding organisational success in a management consultancy firm', paper presented at the Academy of Management Annual Meeting, Denver.

Ambrosini, V. (2002b) 'The resource-based view of the firm', in M. Jenkins and V. Ambrosini (eds), *Strategic Management: A Multiple Perspective Approach*. Basingstoke: Palgrave, pp. 132–52.

Ambrosini, V. and C. Bowman (1997) 'An empirical exploration of tacit knowledge', paper presented at the Strategic Management Society Annual Conference, Barcelona.

Ambrosini, V. and C. Bowman (1998) 'The dilemma of tacit knowledge: tacit routines as a source of sustainable competitive advantage', paper presented at the British Academy of Management, refereed paper track, Nottingham.

Ambrosini, V. and C. Bowman (1999) 'Mapping organisational success', paper presented at the Third International Conference on Organisational Learning, Lancaster, Proceedings, pp. 19–45.

Ambrosini, V. and C. Bowman (2000) 'An empirically derived taxonomy of organisational routines', paper presented at the Academy of Management Annual Meeting, Toronto.

Ambrosini, V. and C. Bowman (2001a) 'Tacit knowledge: some suggestions for operationalisation', *Journal of Management Studies*, vol. 38, no. 6, pp. 811–29.

Ambrosini, V. and C. Bowman (2001b) 'Mapping successful organisational routines', in A. Huff and M. Jenkins (eds) *Mapping Strategic Knowledge*. London: Sage.

Ambrosini, V. and C. Bowman (2002) 'Causal ambiguity: some empirical and conceptual developments', paper presented at the Academy of Management Annual Meeting, Denver.

Amit, R. and P. J. H. Shoemaker (1993) 'Strategic assets and organizational rents', *Strategic Management Journal*, vol. 14, pp. 33–46.

Anderson, J. R. (1983) *The architecture of cognition*. Cambridge, Mass.: Harvard University Press.

Argyris, C. (1996) 'Toward a comprehensive theory of management', in B. Moingeon and A. Edmondson (eds), *Organizational Learning and Competitive Advantage*. London: Sage, pp. 1–6.

Argyris, C. and D. Schön (1974) *Theory in Practice*. San Fransisco: Jossey-Bass.

Asch, S. E. (1952) *Social Psychology*. Englewoods Cliffs, NJ: Prentice-Hall.

Ashford, B. E. and Y. Fried (1988) 'The mindlessness of organisational behaviors', *Human Relations*, vol. 41, pp. 305–29.

Axelrod, R. M. (1976) *The Structure of Decisions: Cognitive Maps of Political Elites*. Princeton, NJ: Princeton University Press.

Badaracco, J. L. (1991) *The Knowledge Link*. Boston, Mass.: Harvard Business School Press.

Baets, W. J. (1998) *Organizational Learning and Knowledge Technologies in a Dynamic Environment*. Boston, Mass.: Kluwer.

Barney, J. B. (1986) 'Organizational culture: can it be a source of sustained competitive advantage?', *Academy of Management Review*, vol. 11, no. 3, pp. 656–65.

Barney, J. B. (1991) 'Firm resources and sustained competitive advantage', *Journal of Management*, vol. 17, no. 1, pp. 99–120.

Barney, J. B. (1995) 'Looking inside for competitive advantage', *Academy of Management Executive*, vol. 9, no. 4, pp. 49–61.

Barney, J. B. (2001) 'Is the resource-based "view" a useful perspective for strategic management research? Yes', *Academy of Management Review*, vol. 26, no. 1, pp. 41–56.

Bartlett, C. A. and S. Ghoshal (1997) 'The myth of the generic manager: New personal competencies for new management roles', *California Management Review*, vol. 40, no. 1, pp. 92–119.

Berry, D. C. (1987) 'The problem of implicit knowledge', *Expert Systems*, vol. 4, no. 3, pp. 144–51.

Berry, D. C. (1994) 'Implicit learning: twenty-five years', *Attention and Performance*, vol. 15, pp. 755–82.

Billsberry, J., V. Ambrosini, J. Moss-Jones and P. Marsh (2001) 'Some suggestions for the application of causal mapping and storytelling to survey individual complementary person-organisation fit', paper presented at the Academy of Management Meeting, Washington DC.

Black, J. A. and K. B. Boal (1994) 'Strategic resources: traits, configurations and paths to sustainable competitive advantage', *Strategic Management Journal*, vol. 15, pp. 131–48.

Blaikie, N. (1993) *Approaches to Social Enquiries*. Cambridge: Polity Press.

Boisot, M. (1998) *Knowledge Assets*. Oxford: Oxford University Press.

Boje, D. M. (1991a) 'Consulting and change in storytelling organisation', *Journal of Organizational Change Management*, vol. 4, no. 3, pp. 7–17.

Boje, D. M. (1991b) 'The storytelling organization: a study of story performance in an office supply firm', *Administrative Science Quarterly*, vol. 36, pp. 106–26.

Bougon, M. G. (1983) 'Uncovering cognitive maps', in G. Morgan (ed.), *Beyond Method*. Beverly Hills, CA: Sage, pp. 173–88.

Bougon, M., N. Baird, J. M. Komocar and W. Ross (1989) 'Identifying strategic loops: the self-Q interviews', in A. S. Huff (ed.), *Managing Strategic Thought*. Chichester: John Wiley, pp. 327–54.

Bougon, M., K. Weick and D. Binkhorst (1977) 'Cognitions in organizations: an analysis of the Utrecht jazz orchestra', *Administrative Science Quarterly*, vol. 22, pp. 606–39.

Bowman, C. (1995) 'Strategy workshops and top team commitment to strategic change', *Journal of Managerial Psychology*, vol. 10, pp. 4–12.

Bowman, C. and V. Ambrosini (1997) 'Perceptions of strategic priorities, consensus and firm performance', *Journal of Management Studies*, vol. 34, no. 2, pp. 241–58.

Bowman, C. and V. Ambrosini (2000a) 'Value creation versus value capture: towards a coherent definition of value in strategy', *British Journal of Management*, vol. 11, pp. 1–15.

Bowman, C. and V. Ambrosini (2000b) 'Strategy from an individual perspective', *European Management Journal*, vol. 18, no. 2, pp. 207–15.

Bowman, C. and V. Ambrosini (2001) '"Value" in the resource-based view of the firm: a contribution to the debate', dialogue paper, *Academy of Management Review*, vol. 26, no. 4, pp. 501–2.

Brown, J. S. and P. Dugruid (1991) 'Organizational learning and communities-of-practice: toward a unified view of working, learning and innovation', *Organization Science*, vol. 2, no. 1, pp. 40–57.

Brown S. L. and K. M. Eisenhardt (1998) *Competing on the Edge, Strategy as Structured Chaos*. Boston, Mass.: Harvard Business School Press.

Brumagim, A. L. (1994) 'A hierarchy of corporate resources', in P. Shrivastava, A. Huff and J. Dutton (eds). *Advances in Strategic Management*, vol. 10, Greenwich, CT: Jai Press, pp. 81–112.

Castanias, R. P. and C. E. Helfat (1991) 'Managerial resources and rents', *Journal of Management*, vol. 17, no. 1, pp. 155–71.

Caves, R. E. (1980) 'Industrial organisation, corporate strategy and structure', *Journal of Economic Literature*, vol. 18, pp. 64–92.

Caves, R. E. and M. Porter (1977) 'From entry barriers to mobility barriers: conjectural decisions and contrived deterrence to new competition', *Quarterly Journal of Economics*, vol. 91, pp. 241–62.

Chatman, J. (1991) 'Matching people and organizations: selection and socialization in public accounting firms', *Administrative Science Quarterly*, vol. 36, pp. 459–84.

Chi, M. T. H., P. J. Feltovich and R. Glaser (1981) 'Categorizations and representation of physics problems by experts and novices', *Cognitive Science*, vol. 5, pp. 121–52.

Clark, K. (1987) 'Investment in new technology and competitive advantage', in D. J. Teece (ed.), *The Competitive Challenge*. Cambridge, Mass.: Ballinger, pp. 59–81.

Clarke, B. (1987) 'Knowledge acquisition for real time knowledge-based systems', Proceedings of the First European Workshop on Knowledge Acquistion for Knowledge-Based Systems, September, Readings, C2.

Cohen, M. D. and P. Bacdayan (1994) 'Organizational routines are stored as procedural memory: evidence from a laboratory study', *Organization Science*, vol. 5, no. 4, pp. 554–68.

Cohen, M. D., R. Burkhart, G. Dosi, M. Edigi, L. Marengo, M. Warglien and S. Winter (1996) 'Routines and other recurring action patterns of organizations: contemporary research issues', *Industrial and Corporate Change*, vol. 5, no. 3, pp. 653–98.

Collis, D. (1991) 'A resource-based analysis of global competition: the case of the bearings industry', *Strategic Management Journal*, vol. 12, pp. 49–68.

Conner, K. R. (1991) 'A historical comparison of resources-based theory and five schools of thought within industrial organisation economics: do we have a new theory of the firm?', *Journal of Management*, vol. 17, no. 1, pp. 121–54.

Conner, K. R. (1994) 'The resource-based challenge to the industry-structure perspective', Best Paper, Proceedings, Annual Meeting of the Academy of Management, Dallas.

Corsini, R. (1987) *Concise Encyclopedia of Psychology*. New York: Wiley.

Cossette, P. and M. Audet (1992) 'Mapping an idiosyncratic schema', *Journal of Management Studies*, vol. 29, no. 3, pp. 325–47.

Crotty, M. (1998) *The Foundations of Social Research*. London: Sage.

Cyert, R. M. and J. G. March (1963) *A Behavioral Theory of the Firm*. Englewood Cliffs, NJ: Prentice-Hall.

Daft, R. L. and K. E. Weick (1984) 'Towards a model of organizations as interpretation systems', *Academy of Management Review*, vol. 9, no. 2, pp. 284–95.

Dierickx, I. and K. Cool (1989) 'Asset stock accumulation and sustainability of competitive advantage', *Management Science*, vol. 35, no. 12, pp. 1504–11.

Dodgson, M. (1993) 'Organizational learning: a review of some literatures', *Organisation Studies*, vol. 14, no. 3, pp. 375–94.

Dougherty, D. (1992) 'Interpretive barriers to successful product innovation in large firms', *Organization Science*, vol. 3, pp. 179–202.

Durkheim, E. (1938) *The Rules of Sociological Method*. New York: Free Press.

Easterby-Smith, M., M. Crossan and D. Nicolini (2000) 'Organizational learning: debates past, present and future', *Journal of Management Studies*, vol. 37, no. 6, pp. 783–96.

Easterby-Smith, M., R. Thorpe and A. Lowe (1992) *Management Research*. London: Sage.

Eden, C. (1990) 'Strategic thinking with computers', *Long Range Planning*, vol. 23, no. 6, pp. 35–43.

Eden, C. (1992) 'On the nature of cognitive maps', *Journal of Management Studies*, vol. 29, no. 3, pp. 261–5.

Eden, C. and F. Ackermann (1998) *Making Strategy*. London: Sage.

Eden, C., F. Ackermann and S. Cropper (1992) 'The analysis of cause maps', *Journal of Management Studies*, vol. 29, no. 3, pp. 309–24.

Eden, C., S. Jones, D. Sims and T. Smithin (1981) 'The intersubjectivity of issues and issues of intersubjectivity', *Journal of Management Studies*, vol. 18, no. 1, pp. 37–47.

Eisenhardt, K. M. (1989) 'Building theories from case study research?', *Academy of Management Review*, vol. 14, no. 4, pp. 532–50.

Elbaz, F. (1983) *Teacher Thinking: A Study of Practical Knowledge*. London: Croom Helm.

Elbaz, F. (1991) 'Research on teachers' knowledge: the evolution of a discourse', *Journal of Curriculum Studies*, vol. 23, no. 1, pp. 1–19.

Eysenck, M. W. and M. T. Keane (1994) *Cognitive Psychology*. Hove: Lawrence Erlbaum.

Flanagan, J. C. (1954) 'The critical incident technique', *Psychological Bulletin*, vol. 51, pp. 327–58.

Fontana, P. A. and J. H. Frey (1994) 'Interviewing: the art of science', in N. K. Denzin and Y. S. Lincoln (eds), *Handbook of Qualitative Research*. Thousand Oaks, CA: Sage, pp. 361–76.

Ford, J. M. and L. E. Wood (1992) 'Structuring and documenting interactions with subject-matter experts', *Performance Improvement Quarterly*, vol. 5, no. 1, pp. 2–24.

Gelwick, R. (1977) *The Way of Discovery*. Oxford: Oxford University Press.

Gharajedaghi, J. and R. L. Ackoff (1994) 'Mechanisms, organisms and social systems', in H. Tsoukas (ed.), *New Thinking in Organizational Behaviour*. Oxford: Butterworth and Heinemann, pp. 25–39.

Giddens, A. (1984) *The Constitution of Society*. Berkeley, CA: University of California Press.

Glaser, R. (1985) 'The nature of expertise', Occasional Paper no. 107. Columbus, Ohio: The National Center for Research in Vocational Education, pp. 1–16.

Grant, R. M. (1991a) 'The resource-based theory of competitive advantage: implications for strategy formulation', *California Management Review*, vol. 33, no. 3, pp. 114–35.

Grant, R. M. (1991b) *Contemporary Strategy Analysis*. Cambridge, Mass.: Basil Blackwell.

Grant, R. M. (1993) 'Organisational capabilities within a knowledge-based view of the firm', paper presented at the annual meeting of the Academy of Management, Atlanta, Georgia.

Grant, R. M. (1996) 'Toward a knowledge-based theory of the firm', *Strategic Management Journal*, vol. 17, pp. 109–22.

Hambrick, D. C. (1994) '1993 presidential address: What of the Academy actually mattered?', *Academy of Management Review*, vol. 19, pp. 11–16.

Hamel, G. and C. K. Prahalad (1994) *Competing for the Future*. Boston, Mass.: Harvard Business School Press.

Hansen, C. D. and W. M. Kahnweiler (1993) 'Storytelling: an instrument for understanding the dynamics of corporate relationships', *Human Relations*, vol. 46, no. 12, pp. 1391–409.

Hardiman, R. J. (1987) 'A naturalistic methodology for knowledge engineering', Proceedings of the First European Workshop on Knowledge Acquistion for Knowledge-Based Systems, September, Readings, E6.

Harré, R. (1984) *The Philosophies of Science*. Oxford: Oxford University Press.

Hatch, M. J. (1997) *Organization Theory: Modern, Symbolic and Postmodern Perspectives*. Oxford: Oxford University Press.

Hedberg, B. (1981) 'How organizations learn and unlearn', in P. C. Nystrom and W. H. Starbuck (eds), *Handbook of organizational learning 1*. Oxford: Oxford University Press, pp. 3–27.

Hedlund, G. (1994) 'A model of knowledge management and the N-form corporation', *Strategic Management Journal*, vol. 15, pp. 73–90.

Henderson, R. and I. Cockburn (1994) 'Measuring competence? Exploring firm effects in pharmaceutical research', *Strategic Management Journal*, vol. 15, pp. 63–84.

Hill, R. C. and M. Levenhagen (1995) 'Metaphors and mental models: sense-making and sensegiving in innovative and entrepreneurial activities', *Journal of Management*, vol. 21, no. 6, pp. 1057–74.

Hodgkin, R. A. (1992) 'Michael Polanyi on the activity of knowing – the bearing of his ideas on the theory of multiple intelligence', *Oxford Review of Education*, vol. 18, no. 3, pp. 253–67.

Hu, Y. S. (1995) 'The international transferability of the firm's advantages', *California Management Review*, vol. 37, no. 4, pp. 73–88.

Hubbart, G. and P. Bromiley (1994) 'Researchers and top managers: how do they measure firm performance?', paper presented at the Academy of Management Meetings, Dallas.

Huff, A. S. (1990) 'Mapping strategic thought', in A. S. Huff (ed.), *Mapping Strategic Thought*. Chichester: John Wiley, pp. 11–49.

Hunt, S. D. (1995) 'The resource-advantage theory of competition: towards explaining productivity and economic growth', *Journal of Management Inquiry*, vol. 4, no. 4, pp. 317–32.

Ireland, R. D., M. A. Hitt, M. Camp and D. L. Sexton (2001) 'Integrating entre-preneurship and strategic management actions to create firm wealth', *Academy of Management Journal*, vol. 15, no. 1, pp. 49–63.

Jacobsen, R. (1988) 'The persistence of abnormal returns', *Strategic Management Journal*, vol. 9, pp. 41–58.

Jelinek, M. (1979) *Institutionalizing Innovation*. New York: Praeger.

Jenkins, M. (1995) 'Subjective strategies for small business growth: an evaluation of the causal maps of small independent retailers', unpublished PhD dissert-ation, Cranfield SOM.

Jenkins, M. (1998) 'Theory and practice of comparing causal maps', in C. Eden and J. C. Spender (eds), *Managerial and organisational cognition*. London: Sage, pp. 231–57.

Jensen, A. R. (1993) 'Test validity: g versus tacit knowledge', *Current Directions in Psychological Science*, vol. 1, pp. 9–10.

Johnson, G. (1988) 'Rethinking incrementalism', *Strategic Management Journal*, vol. 9, no. 1, pp. 75–91.

Johnson, G. and K. Scholes (1993, 1997) *Exploring Corporate Strategy*. London: Prentice-Hall.

Johnson, M. (1989) 'Embodied knowledge', *Curriculum Inquiry*, vol. 19, no. 4, pp. 361–77.

Johnson, P. E. (1983) 'What kind of expert should a system be', *Journal of Medicine and Philosophy*, vol. 8, pp. 77–97.

Judge, W. Q. and A. Miller (1991) 'Antecedents and outcomes of decision speed in different environments', *Academy of Management Journal*, vol. 34, no. 2, pp. 449–64.

Kamann, D. J. F. (1998) 'Modelling networks: a long way to go to the triple plus methodology', Proceedings of the Fourteenth IMP Annual Conference, vol. 3, pp. 61–85.

Kerlinger, F. N. (1973) *Foundations of Behavioral Research*. New York: Holt-Saunders.

Kerlinger, F. N. (1998) *Foundations of Behavioral Research*. New York: Holt-Saunders.

Klimecki, R. and H. Lassleben (1998) 'Modes of organizational learning', *Management Learning*, vol. 29, no. 4, pp. 405–30.

Kogut, B. and U. Zander (1992) 'Knowledge of the firm, combinative capabilities, and the replication of technology', *Organisation Science*, vol. 3, pp. 383–96.

Lam, A. (1997) 'Embedded firms, embedded knowledge: problems of collaboration and knowledge transfer in global cooperative ventures', *Organization Science*, vol. 18, no. 6, pp. 973–96.

Lam, A. (2000) 'Tacit knowledge, organizational learning and societal institutions: an integrated framework', *Organization Studies*, vol. 21, no. 3, pp. 487–513.

Langfield-Smith, K. (1992) 'Exploring the need for a shared map', *Journal of Management Studies*, vol. 29, no. 3, pp. 349–68.

Langlois, R. N. (1995) 'Capabilities and coherence in firms and markets', in C. A. Montgomery (ed.), *Resource-Based and Evolutionary Theories of the Firm: Towards a Synthesis*. Boston, Mass.: Kluwer, pp. 71–100.

Laukkanen, M. (1994) 'Comparative cause mapping of organizational cognitions', *Organization Science*, vol. 5, no. 3, pp. 322–43.

Laukkannen, M. (1998) 'Conducting causal mapping research', in C. Eden and J. C. Spender (eds), *Managerial and Organisational Cognition*. London: Sage, pp. 168–91.

Leonard-Barton, D. (1992) 'Core capabilities and core rigidities: a paradox in managing new product development', *Strategic Management Journal*, vol. 13, pp. 111–26.

Levitt, B. and J. G. March (1988) 'Organizational learning', *Annual Review of Sociology*, vol. 14, pp. 319–40.

Lippman, S. A. and R. P. Rumelt (1982) 'Uncertain imitability: an analysis of interfirm differences in efficiency under competition', *The Bell Journal of Economics*, vol. 13, no. 2, pp. 418–38.

Louis, M. R. and J. M. Bartunek (1992) 'Insider/outsider research teams: collaboration across diverse perspectives', *Journal of Management Inquiry*, vol. 1, no. 2, pp. 101–10.

Lyles, M. A. and C. R. Schwenk (1992) 'Top management, strategy and organisational knowledge structures', *Journal of Management Studies*, vol. 29, no. 2, pp. 155–74.

Mahoney, J. T. and Pandian J. R. (1992) 'The resource-based view within the conversation of strategic management', *Strategic Management Journal*, vol. 13, pp. 363–80.

Maijoor, S. and A. Van Witteloostuijn (1996) 'An empirical test of the resource-based theory: strategic regulation in the Dutch audit industry', *Strategic Management Journal*, vol. 17, pp. 549–69.

March, J. G. (1991) 'Exploration and exploitation in organizational learning', *Organization Science*, vol. 2, no. 10, pp. 71–87.

March, J. G. and J. P. Olsen (1976) *Ambiguity and Choice in Organisations*. Bergen: Universitetforlaget.

Markóczy, L. and J. Goldberg (1995) 'A method for eliciting and comparing causal maps', *Journal of Management*, vol. 21, no. 2, pp. 305–33.

Martin, J. (1982) 'Stories and scripts in organizational settings', in A. H. Hastorf and A. M. Isen (eds), *Cognitive Social Psychology*. New York: Elsevier, pp. 255–305.

Masters, R. S. W. (1992) 'Knowledge, knerves and know-how: the role of explicit vs. implicit knowledge in the breakdown of a complex motor skill under pressure', *British Journal of Psychology*, vol. 83, pp. 343–58.

Miller, D. (1988) 'Relating Porter's business strategies to environment and structure: analysis and performance implications', *Academy of Management Journal*, vol. 31, pp. 280–308.

Miller, D. (1996) 'A preliminary typology of organizational learning: synthesising the literature', *Journal of Management*, vol. 22, no. 3, pp. 485–505.

Miller, D. and J. Shamsie (1996) 'The resource-based view of the firm in two environments: the Hollywood film studios from 1936 to 1965', *Academy of Management Journal*, vol. 39, no. 3, pp. 519–43.

Mintzberg, H. (1979) *The Structuring of Organizations: A Synthesis of the Research*. Englewood Cliffs, NJ: Prentice-Hall.

Mintzberg, H. (1983) *Structure in Fives: Designing Effective Organizations*. Englewood Cliffs, NJ: Prentice-Hall.

Mintzberg, H., D. Raisinghani and A. Théorêt (1976) 'The structure of "unstructured" decision processes', *Administrative Science Quarterly*, vol. 21, pp. 246–75.

Mosakowski, E. (1993) 'A resource-based perspective on the dynamic strategy – performance relationship: an empirical examination of the focus and differentiation strategies in entrepreneurial firms', *Journal of Management*, vol. 19, no. 4, pp. 819–39.

Mosakowski, E. (1997) 'Managerial prescriptions under the resource-based view of strategy: the example of motivational techniques', *Strategic Management Journal*, vol. 19, no. 12, pp. 1169–82.

Munby, H. (1986) 'Metaphor in the thinking of teachers: an exploratory study', *Journal of Curriculum Studies*, vol. 18, no. 2, pp. 197–209.

Nelson, R. E. and K. M. Mathews (1991) 'Cause maps and social network analysis in organisational diagnosis', *Journal of Applied Behavioral Science*, vol. 27, pp. 379–97.

Nelson, R. R. and S. G. Winter (1982) *An Evolutionary Theory of Economic Change*. Cambridge, Mass.: Belknap Press.

Nonaka, I. (1991) 'The knowledge-creating company', *Harvard Business Review*, vol. 69, no. 6, pp. 96–104.

Nonaka, I. and N. Konno (1998) 'The concept of "ba": building a foundation for knowledge creation', *California Management Review*, vol. 40, no. 3, pp. 40–54.

Nonaka, I. and H. Takeuchi (1995) *The Knowledge-Creating Company*. Oxford: Oxford University Press.

Ogbonna, E. (1993) 'Managing organisational culture: fantasy or reality?', *Human Resource Management Journal*, vol. 3, no. 2, pp. 42–54.

O'Reilly, C. A., J. Chatman and D. F. Caldwell (1991) 'People and organizational culture: A profile comparison approach to assessing person–organization fit', *Academy of Management Journal*, vol. 34, pp. 487–516.

Ortony, A. (1975) 'Why metaphors are necessary and not just nice', *Educational Theory*, vol. 25, no. 1, pp. 45–53.

Pavitt, K. (1991) 'Key characteristics of the large innovating firm', *British Journal of Management*, vol. 2, pp. 41–50.

Penrose, E. T. (1959) *The Theory of Growth of the Firm*. New York: Wiley.

Pentland, B. T. and H. H. Rueter (1994) 'Organizational routines and grammar of action', *Administrative Science Quarterly*, vol. 39, no. 3, pp. 484–510.

Peteraf, M. A. (1993) 'The cornerstone of competitive advantage: a resource-based view', *Strategic Management Journal*, vol. 14, pp. 179–91.

Peters, T. J. (1984) 'Strategy follows structure: developing distinctive skills', in G. Carroll and D. Vogel (eds), *Strategy and Organization*. Mansfield: Pitman.

Pettigrew, A. M. (1973) *The Politics of Organizational Decision Making*. London: Tavistock.

Pfeffer, J. (1995) 'Producing sustainable competitive advantage through the effective management of people', *Academy of Management Executive*, vol. 9, no. 1, pp. 55–69.

Pfeffer, J. and J. F. Veiga (1999) 'Putting people first for organizational success', *Academy of Management Executive*, vol. 13, no. 2, pp. 37–48.

Polanyi, M. (1962) *Personal Knowledge, Towards a Post Critical Philosophy*. London: Routledge and Kegan Paul.

Polanyi, M. (1966) *The Tacit Dimension*. New York: Doubleday.

Polanyi, M. (1976) 'Tacit knowing', in M. H. Marx and F. E. Goodson (eds), *Theories in Contemporary Psychology*, 2nd edn. New York: MacMillan, pp. 330–44.

Porter, M. E. (1980) *Competitive Strategy: Techniques for Analysing Industries and Competitors*. New York: Free Press.

Porter, M. E. (1985) *Competitive Advantage: Creating and Sustaining Superior Performance*. New York: Free Press.

Prahalad, C. K. and G. Hamel (1990) 'The core competence of the corporation', *Harvard Business Review*, vol. 68, no. 3, pp. 79–91.

Priem, R. L. and J. E. Butler (2001) 'Is the resource-based "view" a useful perspective for strategic management research?', *Academy of Management Review*, vol. 26, no. 1, pp. 22–40.

Quinn, J. B. (1992) *The Intelligent Enterprise: A Knowledge and Service-Based Paradigm for Industry*. New York: Free Press.

Rao, H. (1994) 'The social construction of reputation: certification contests, legitimation, and the survival of organizations in the American automobile industry: 1895–1912', *Strategic Management Journal*, vol. 15, pp. 29–44.

Ravetz, J. R. (1971) *Scientific Knowledge and its Social Problems*. Oxford: Clarendon Press.

Reason, P. and J. Rowan (1981) *Human Inquiry: A Sourcebook of New Paradigm Research*. Chichester: Wiley.

Reber, A. S. (1989) 'Implicit learning and tacit knowledge', *Journal of Experimental Psychology*, vol. 118, pp. 219–35.

Reed, R. and R. J. DeFillipi (1990) 'Causal ambiguity, barriers to imitation and sustainable competitive advantage', *Academy of Management Review*, vol. 15, no. 1, pp. 88–102.

Reed, S. K. (1996) *Cognition*. Pacific Grove, CA: Brooks/Cole.

Reichheld, F. F. (1996), 'Learning from customer defections', *Harvard Business Review*, vol. 74, no. 2, pp. 56–69.

Rouse, M. J. and U. S. Daellenbach (1999) 'Rethinking research methods for the resource-based perspective: isolating sources of sustainable competitive advantage', *Strategic Management Journal*, vol. 20, no. 5, pp. 487–94.

Rumelt, R. (1984) 'Toward a strategic theory of the firm', in R. Lamb (ed.), *Competitive Strategic Management*. Englewoods Cliffs, NJ: Prentice-Hall, pp. 556–70.

Rumelt, R. (1987) 'Theory, strategy and entrepreneurship', in D. J. Teece (ed.), *The Competitive Challenge*. Cambridge, Mass.: Ballinger, pp. 137–58.

Ryle, G. (1949) *The Concept of Mind*. London: Hutchinson.

Sackmann, S. (1989) 'The role of metaphors in organization transformation', *Human Relations*, vol. 42, no. 6, pp. 463–85.

Schein, E. H. (1985) *Organizational Culture and Leadership*. San Fransisco: Jossey-Bass.

Schein, E. H. (1992) 'Coming to a new awareness of organization culture', in G. Salaman (ed.), *Human Resources Strategies*. London: Sage, pp. 237–53.

Schiffman, L. G. and L. L. Kanuk (1991) *Consumer Behavior*. Englewood Cliffs, NJ: Prentice-Hall.

Schön, D. (1983) 'Organizational learning', in G. Morgan (ed.), *Beyond Method*. Beverly Hills, CA: Sage, pp. 114–28.

Schön, D. (1987) *Educating the Reflective Practitioner*. San Fransisco: Jossey-Bass.

Schön, D. (1994) 'Teaching artistry through refelection in action', in H. Tsoukas (ed.), *New Thinking in Organizational Behaviour*. Oxford: Butterworth and Heinemann, pp. 235–49.

Selznick, P. (1957) *Leadership in Administration: A Sociological Interpretation*. New York: Harper & Row.

Sheetz, S. D., D. P. Tegarden, K. A. Kozar and I. Zigurs (1994) 'A group support systems approach to cognitive mapping', *Journal of Management Information Systems*, vol. 11, no. 1, pp. 31–57.

Shirley, D. A. and J. Langan-Fox (1996) 'Intuition: a review of the literature', *Psychological Reports*, vol. 79, pp. 563–84.

Silverman, D (1993) *Interpreting Qualitative Data*. London: Sage.

Sobol, M. G. and D. Lei (1994) 'Environment, manufacturing technology and embedded knowledge', *International Journal of Human Factors in Manufacturing*, vol. 4, no. 2, pp. 167–89.

Sparrow, J. (1998) *Knowledge in Organisations*. London: Sage.

Spender, J. C. (1989) *Industry Recipes: The Nature and Sources of Managerial Judgement*. Oxford: Basil Blackwell.

Spender, J. C. (1993) 'Competitive advantage from tacit knowledge? Unpacking the concept and its strategic implication', Best Paper, Proceedings, Annual Meeting of the Academy of Management, Atlanta, Georgia.

Spender, J. C. (1994) 'Organisational knowledge, collective practice and Penrose rents', *International Business Review*, vols 3–4, pp. 1–5.

Spender, J. C. (1996) 'Competitive advantage from tacit knowledge? Unpacking the concept and its strategic implications', in B. Moingeon and A. Edmondson (eds), *Organizational Learning and Competitive Advantage*. London: Sage, pp. 56–73.

Spender, J. C. and P. Baumard (1995) 'Turning troubled firms around: case evidence for a Penrosian account of strategic recovery', paper presented at the Academy of Management Annual Conference, Vancouver, Canada.

Srivastava, S. and F. J. Barrett (1988) 'The transforming nature of metaphors in group development: a study in group theory', *Human Relations*, vol. 41, no. 1, pp. 31–64.

Sternberg, R. J. (1994) 'Tacit knowledge and job success', in N. Anderson and P. Herriot (eds), *Assessment and Selection in Organizations: Methods and Practice for Recruitment and Appraisal*. London: John Wiley and Sons, pp. 27–39.

Sternberg, R. J. (1995) 'Theory and measurement of tacit knowledge as a part of practical intelligence', *Zeitschrift fur Psychologie*, vol. 203, pp. 319–34.

Sternberg, R. J., R. K. Wagner, W. M. Williams and J. A. Horvath (1995) 'Testing common sense', *American Psychologist*, vol. 50, no. 11, pp. 912–27.

Stevenson, R. J. (1993) *Language, Thought and Representation*. Chichester: John Wiley and Sons.

Teece, D. J. (1990) 'Economic analysis: contributions and impediments', in J. W. Fredrickson (ed.), *Perspectives on Strategic Management*. New York: Harper, pp. 39–80.

Teece, D. J. (2000) 'Strategies for managing knowledge assets; the role of firm structure and industrial context', *Long Range Planning*, vol. 33, no. 1, pp. 35–54.

Teece, D. J., G. Pisano and A. Shuen (1997) 'Dynamic capabilities and strategic management', *Strategic Management Journal*, vol. 18, no. 7, pp. 509–33.

Thomas, H. and T. Pollock (1999) 'From IO economics' SCP paradigm through strategic groups to competence-based competition: reflections on the puzzle of competitive strategy', *British Journal of Management*, vol. 10, pp. 127–40.

Thomas, W. I. and D. S. Thomas (1928) *The Child in America: Behaviour, Problems and Progress*. New York: Knopf.

Tranfield, D. and S. Smith (1998) 'The strategic regeneration of manufacturing by changing routines', *International Journal of Operations and Production Management*, vol. 18, no. 2, pp. 114–29.

Tsoukas, H. (1991) 'The missing link: a transformational view of metaphors in organizational science', *Academy of Management Review*, vol. 16, no. 3, pp. 566–85.

Tulving, E. (1985) 'How many different memory systems are there?', *American Psychologist*, vol. 40, no. 1, pp. 385–98.

Vaughan, F. E. (1979) *Awakening Intuition*. New York: Anchor Press/Doubleday.

Verdin, P. J. and P. J. Williamson (1994) 'Core competences, competitive advantage and market analysis: forging the links', in G. Hamel and A. Heene (eds), *Competence-Based Competition*. Chichester: John Wiley and Sons, pp. 77–110.

Wagner, R. K. (1987) 'Tacit knowledge in everyday intelligent behavior', *Journal of Personality and Social Psychology*, vol. 52, no. 6, pp. 1236–47.

Wagner, R. K. and R. J. Sternberg (1985) 'Practical intelligence in real-world pursuits: the role of tacit knowledge', *Journal of Personality and Social Psychology*, vol. 49, no. 2, pp. 436–58.

Wagner, R. K. and R. J. Sternberg (1986) 'Tacit knowledge and intelligence in the everyday world', in R. K. Wagner and R. J. Sternberg (eds), *Practical Intelligence*. Cambridge: Cambridge University Press, pp. 51–83.

Wagner, R. K. and R. J. Sternberg (1991) 'Tacit knowledge: its uses in identifying, assessing and developing managerial talent', in J. W. Jones, B. D. Steffy and D. W. Bray (eds), *Applying Psychology in Business*. New York: Lexington Books, pp. 333–44.

Walsh, J. P. (1988) 'Selectivity and selective perception – an investigation of managers' belief structures and information processing', *Academy of Management Journal*, vol. 31, no. 4, pp. 873–93.

Walsh, J. P. and G. R. Ungson (1991) 'Organizational memory', *Academy of Management Review*, vol. 16, pp. 57–91.

Waugh, N. C. and D. Norman (1965) 'Primary memory', *Psychology Review*, vol. 72, pp. 89–104.

Weick, K. E. and M. G. Bougon (1986) 'Organizations as cognitive maps', in H. P. Sims (ed.), *The Thinking Organization*. San Fransisco, CA: Jossey-Bass, pp. 102–35.

Weick, K. E. and K. H. Roberts (1993) 'Collective mind in organizations: heedful interrelating on flight decks', *Administrative Science Quarterly*, vol. 38, pp. 357–81.

Werner, O. and G. M. Schoepfle (1987) *Systematic Fieldwork*, vol. 1. Newbury Park, CA: Sage.

Wernerfelt, B. (1984) 'A resource-based view of the firm', *Strategic Management Journal*, vol. 5, pp. 171–80.

Westley, F. and J. A. Waters (1988) 'Group Facilitation Skills for Managers', *Management Education and Development*, vol. 19, no. 2, pp. 134–43.

Wilcox King, A. and C. P. Zeithaml (2001) 'Competencies and firm performance: examining the causal ambiguity paradox', *Strategic Management Journal*, vol. 22, pp. 75–99.

Wilkins, A. L. and M. P. Thompson (1991) 'On getting the story crooked (and straight)', *Journal of Organizational Change Management*, vol. 4, no. 3, pp. 18–26.

Winter, S. G. (1987) 'Knowledge and competence as strategic assets', in D. J. Teece (ed.), *The Competitive Challenge*. Cambridge, Mass.: Ballinger, pp. 159–84.

Winter, S. G. (1995) 'Four Rs of profitability: rents, resources, routines, and replication', in C. A Montgomery (ed.), *Resource-Based and Evolutionary Theories of the Firm: Towards a Synthesis*. Boston, Mass.: Kluwer, pp. 147–78.

Wright, R. W. (1994) 'The effects of tacitness and tangibility on the diffusion of knowledge-based resources', Best Paper, Proceedings, Annual Meeting of the Academy of Management, Dallas.

Yinger, R. J. (1986) 'Examining thought in action: a theoretical and methodological critique of research on interactive teaching', *Teaching and Teacher Education*, vol. 2, no. 3, pp. 263–83.

# Index